Fast, Easy, and In Cash

Fast, Easy, and In Cash

Artisan Hardship and Hope in the Global Economy

JASON ANTROSIO AND
RUDI COLLOREDO-MANSFELD

The University of Chicago Press ❋ *Chicago and London*

Jason Antrosio is associate professor of anthropology at Hartwick College in Oneonta, New York. Rudi Colloredo-Mansfeld is professor and chair of anthropology at the University of North Carolina, Chapel Hill.

The University of Chicago Press, Chicago 60637
The University of Chicago Press, Ltd., London
© 2015 by The University of Chicago
All rights reserved. Published 2015.
Printed in the United States of America

24 23 22 21 20 19 18 17 16 15   1 2 3 4 5

ISBN-13: 978-0-226-30258-4 (cloth)
ISBN-13: 978-0-226-30261-4 (paper)
ISBN-13: 978-0-226-30275-1 (e-book)
DOI: 10.7208/chicago/9780226302751.001.0001

Library of Congress Cataloging-in-Publication Data

Antrosio, Jason, author.
    Fast, easy, and in cash : artisan hardship and hope in the global economy / Jason Antrosio and Rudi Colloredo-Mansfeld.
        pages ; cm
    Includes bibliographical references and index.
    ISBN 978-0-226-30258-4 (cloth : alk. paper) — ISBN 978-0-226-30261-4 (pbk. : alk. paper) — ISBN 978-0-226-30275-1 (ebook) 1. Artisans—Andes Region. 2. Artisans—Andes Region—Economic conditions. 3. Cottage industries—Andes Region. 4. Andes Region—Economic conditions—21st century. I. Colloredo-Mansfeld, Rudolf Josef, 1965– author. II. Title.
    HD9999.H363A63 2015
    331.7'94—dc23
                                    2015007905

For our children,

Sabrina and Sam
—JA

Sky, Mia, and Zoe
—RCM

Contents

Acknowledgments

Half a world away from the Andean towns of this research lies the great Kumasi Central Market in Ghana. The anthropologist Gracia Clark has written at length about the "dynamism and unruliness" of Kumasi Central Market, where in the 1980s some twenty thousand traders worked daily selling food, services, crafts, and imports. Seventy percent of these operators were women. Their stalls, tables, and stores spread in "a living carpet of energetic, even desperate commercial initiative" (Clark 1994, 1). Yet the Kumasi Central Market was also the place where young mothers worked in a committed but less frenetic way. They undertook what was called Nursing Mother Work. These were market niches women created to provide a reliable income during a crucial phase of a woman's life when the urgency of work is driven on by the urgency of caring for an infant or toddler. But childcare and market work were not in conflict—child care and work went together, as mothers found their place in the street or market, selling with a new sense of purpose. In Clark's phrase, "motherhood demands work, even if it constrains it" (1999, 723).

Clark's work and phrasings came to mind as we pursued this research, went to conferences, and wrote up our results. Sometimes she came to mind for her creativity. Clark often collaborated with women who worked in Andean marketplaces, like

Florence Babb, Linda Seligmann, and Mary Weismantel, who were doing incredibly innovative research on markets, gender, and identity. For those of us documenting agrarian economies in the 1990s, it seemed as if they were working in color at a time when economic anthropology was being churned out in black and white.

The idea of Nursing Mother Work also resonated because our own research had become a kind of father's work, an occupation that in its own way was both urgent and constrained. As we began a collaborative project in 2004, we were both husbands and fathers. Our spouses literally had to secure Nursing Mother Work as they launched careers in the college towns where we had landed, on the fortunate side of the academic job market (which looked more and more like the winner-take-all payout described in chapter 3). Our children were toddlers or infants, or on the horizon, as we mapped out a comparative project for Otavalo and Atuntaqui. Up to this point in our careers, our writing had drawn on doctoral fieldwork involving the classic solo, immersive ethnographic techniques that have long marked anthropology: living in the research community, joining in work and daily domestic life, dashing off to a community meeting, town festival, or weekly market, and so on. Now, we had teaching jobs, children, and working spouses.

Only by teaming up would we be able to tackle the economic issues unfolding in these Andean towns. Usually our research periods in Ecuador were measured in weeks, not months. And if we were lucky enough to have our families with us during our research, our days would be split between research and family outings. To capture the social, cultural, and political implications of the economic changes we tracked, we needed to find new ways to participate in the flow of action in Otavalo, Atuntaqui, and elsewhere. The solutions we found became integral to understanding the stories in the chapters that follow.

In part, we had to be patient and parcel out our work over several summers and multiple return trips. We also grew to rely on a diverse set of collaborators, institutions, and research assistants.

Together these collaborations and regular returns helped reveal how the innovations and disruptions that we documented in our initial research rapidly evolved. Thus, in Atuntaqui, we sought to improve our list of family firms in the casual clothing business by going out to find the enterprises that showed up on various economic development reports. Working with the chamber of commerce to recruit a field assistant from Atuntaqui, we partnered with Byron Beltran in 2006 to develop a map of the store and workshop locations. By returning to Atuntaqui and reconnecting with Byron three more times over the following five years, we were able to update the map and show how rapidly investment in apparel was reshaping the center of the city. And in Otavalo in 2004, we worked with the Union of Indigenous Artisans of the Centenario Market-Otavalo (la Unión de Artesanos Indígenas del Mercado Centenario-Otavalo, or UNAIMCO) to hire two research assistants, Myriam Campo and Toa Maldonado, to help with a producer survey focusing on fashion and cultural identity in designs. The original purpose in 2004 was to identify whether trades that had a strong cultural identity were more economically resilient. Working with Toa and others on return visits in 2005, 2006, and 2007, we tracked the ongoing life of the original designs. The longitudinal study gave us more insight into both innovation and the identity of the marketplace. Steady, committed, part time, collaborative, and long term was our modus operandi as fathers and, if it felt a constrained kind of ethnography, it also turned out to be very fruitful.

In Atuntaqui, officers and staff at the Chamber of Commerce of Antonio Ante (CCAA) supported our efforts year in and year out beginning in 2005. Diego Lopez, the director of the CCAA in 2004, helped forge our original connections, and his successor Santiago Salgado invited us to meetings, helped us recruit research assistants, and facilitated introductions to business operators. Diego Salgado, who served on the CCAA board, took the time to talk us through the issues they faced as they pursued more ambitious promotional events. And perhaps the most impactful support and advice came from Lili Posso, who worked her way up from secretary to director of the CCAA over the years of our project. Lili provided both crucial logistical support for our surveys and incisive commentary about the social world interwoven with the economic programs unfolding in Atuntaqui in the 2000s.

Several businesses became our "go-to" locations for reality checks—moments to see how Atuntaqui's economic and cultural projects were playing out in the lives of manufacturers. At these operations, Angelo Placencia, Gabriela Vega, and Fabian Marroquin generously spent time with us explaining their businesses and lives. They shared not just successes but also their setbacks, including a heartbreaking account that stays with us to this day.

When our research turned toward the hulking industrial plant of the Fábrica Imbabura and its legacy among contemporary producers, we found strong allies within Atuntaqui's municipal government. The director of Culture and Tourism, Mauricio Ayala, together with Fany Paredes, had a vision to recover the factory as a museum and heritage site, and also to record the words and memories of long-retired workers. They enlisted our project in that effort and their guidance helped us to see how the trades at the center of our research grew from the town's history.

We are especially grateful to the protagonists in the story of President Rafael Correa's embroidered shirts—Alicia Cisneros, Sandra Meza, and Teresa Casa—for taking time to talk with us. Each in their own way widened our understanding of the production of Correa's garment by sharing their own professional story and the communities that have shaped their practice.

In Otavalo, UNAIMCO has served as our counterpart, advisor, and logistical base since 2001. The union's presidents, Lic. Jose Manuel Quimbo, Lic. Segundo Maldonado, and Lic. Jose Antonio Lema, and longtime board member Arq. Humberto Lema helped shape the questions of our research as they grappled with how the union could support innovation and design creativity. Ruth Ceron, UNAIMCO's secretary, was a wonderful administrator as we recruited and employed research assistants for this partnership.

From 2001 to 2007, we worked with five outstanding field re-searchers: Blanca Arellano, Myriam Campo, Nelly Maigua, Toa Maldonado, and Adriana Muñuela. Among them, they helped us execute eleven surveys, interview tasks, and mapping efforts: Dollarization Impact Interviews (2001), Acrylic Fiber Sweater Sales Spot Check Survey (2001), Inter-workshop Knitting Machinery Inventory (2001), Culture and Fashion Design Survey (2004), Cotton Shirt Producer Survey (2004), Design Imitation and Innovation Interviews (2005), UNAIMCO Fashion and Training Survey (2005), Follow-up UNAIMCO Fashion and Training Survey (2006), Acrylic Sweater and Cotton Shirt Marketplace Design Detail Census (2006), Artisan Apparel and Textile Production Survey and Map (2006), and Monthly Displayed Design Detail Census (2006–07). Without their expertise, efficiency, organization, and senses of humor, we would not have been able to gather the material at the heart of our analysis.

As we updated the material on Tigua painting, Luis Cuyo Cuyo, Purificación Cuyo, and Alfredo Toaquiza continued to fill us in on the scope of their work. In 2013 and 2014, painters in Quilotoa, including José Pilatasig, Nelson Pilatasig, and José Guamangate, explained new issues that have come up in the economics of Tigua painting.

As the threads of a decade of work on artisans came together in a book project, we approached T. David Brent at the University of Chicago Press. A spirited pitch session at the annual meetings of the American Anthropological Association taught us how best to cast the argument. The anonymous reviewers recruited by the press provided exceptionally constructive and detailed feedback on everything from Ecuadorian handicraft chronologies to the suitability of Bourdieu's ideas for understanding artisan competition. We hope that they see the value of their efforts here, and we absolve them of responsibility for any errors that might remain. Priya Nelson's work to secure these reviewers, her insightful guidance to revise the manuscript, and her regular encouragement maintained the momentum of this project. We count ourselves lucky to be among her first authors as she widens her role at the press. Stimulating conversations with Paolo Bocci about his project on invasive species in the Galapagos inspired our thinking about invasive trades in artisan economies. At Priya's suggestion, we sought out a biologist, Professor John Bruno at UNC Chapel Hill, to orient our understanding of invasive species and how they may serve as a model for invasive trades. John helpfully pointed out where we could add precision to our language and offered us some useful articles.

Principle fieldwork for this project began in 2004 and several institutions provided important funding to ensure continuity in the work. For Rudi Colloredo-Mansfeld, the University of Iowa provided an International Programs International Summer Research Fellowship (2004) and Faculty Scholar Award (2005–07), which enabled the pilot funding and research leaves to develop the project. A Fulbright Award from the CIES program made possible six months of research in 2006. In 2010, the National Science Foundation funded "The Market as a Commons Workshop: Developing a Comparative Framework for Investigating Cultural Resources in Regional Economies" (#BCS-0966609), which allowed us to bring together a number of researchers working on similar issues and refine the arguments that we offer in this book. More recently, the Wenner Gren Foundation funded a proposal developed with Dr. Diego Quiroga of Universidad San Francisco de Quito, "Territories, Stewardship, and Place-Based Economies in Andean Communities: Building Participatory Research Capacity" (2013), which enabled follow-up research among the artists of Tigua.

In Quito a number of colleagues have been terrific partners over the years, not only supporting the work but helping to understand the transformation underway in Ecuador in this epoch of Rafael Correa's presidency. Carlos de la Torre and Carmen Martinez Novo have provided invaluable and regular insights on the changing culture of the country and how the current president's politics filter through Ecuadorian society. Recently, anthropologists at the Universidad de San Francisco-Quito who have been working on the economies and territory project—Diego Quiroga, Julie Williams, Angelica Ordonez, and Michael Hill—have helped to develop creative ways to pursue research on community economies.

For Jason Antrosio, primary research support came from Hartwick College Faculty Research Grants for fieldwork in 2005, 2006, 2009, and 2011. Hartwick College also offered time and writing support through a Wandersee Scholar-in-Residence Fellowship (2007–08) and an Endowed Hardy Chair Professorship (2010–13). The National Endowment for the Humanities Summer Institute, "Teaching the History of Political Economy," at Duke University (2010) was an invaluable source for retracing critical ideas in political economy.

One of the wonderful parts of this extended fieldwork was being able to reconnect—albeit too quickly and briefly—with a previous research area in southwestern Colombia and especially to revisit Túquerres. Maruja Rojas and the Portilla family were, as always, wonderful and generous hosts, and they helped overview the rise and fall of a speculative pyramid-finance scheme that rocked the entire north Andean region.

Finally, we return to where we started: this has been father's work. The longer periods of field research were only possible because our spouses were able to organize their own work to allow whole families to relocate, or to keep the home base running at a pace that echoed the artisan families we document in this book. Rudi's spouse, Chesca Colloredo-Mansfeld, has in recent years managed to direct from a kitchen table in Ecuador the international work of miraclefeet, a nonprofit working in more than ten countries to support the treatment of clubfoot. Jason's spouse, Sallie Han, is now an anthropologist researching pregnancy, childhood, and the very kinds of Nursing Mother Work discussed by Gracia Clark. All of our children have been to Ecuador in diapers, and now have grown into research assistants and para-anthropologists. They too now badger us about getting our results published or berating how much writing and teaching anthropology seems to have become "screen time." We are extraordinarily lucky to be able to share this life and pursuit with them—perhaps in the end, like the artisans in this book, this anthropology is family work.

Chapters 2, 3, 4, 5, and 6 contain material that has previously been published and we gratefully acknowledge permission granted by the following publications and collaborators:

Chapter 2: Jason Antrosio and Rudi Colloredo-Mansfeld, "Risk-Seeking Peasants, Excessive Artisans: Speculation in the Northern Andes," *Economic Anthropology* 1, no. 1 (2014): 124–38.

Chapter 3: Rudi Colloredo-Mansfeld, "An Ethnography of Neoliberalism: Understanding Competition in Artisan Economies," *Current Anthropology* 43, no. 1 (2002): 113–37.

Chapters 4 and 5: Rudi Colloredo-Mansfeld, Jason Antrosio, and Eric C. Jones, "Creativity, Place, and Commodities: The Making of Public Economies in Andean Apparel Industries," in *Textile Economies: Power and Value from the Local to the Transnational*, eds. Walter E. Little and Patricia A. McAnany (Lanham, MD: AltaMira Press, 2011): 39–55. Eric Jones helped us pursue two-mode network analysis in this original chapter that revealed the way different designs connected various enterprises. While we have not included his visualizations here, his work has informed our understanding of how producers group together through their designs.

Chapter 5: Rudi Colloredo-Mansfeld and Jason Antrosio, "Economic Clusters or Cultural Commons? The Limits of Competition-Driven Development in the Ecuadorian Andes," *Latin American Research Review* 44, no. 1 (2009): 132–57.

Prologue and Chapter 6: Rudi Colloredo-Mansfeld, Paola Mantilla, and Jason Antrosio, "Rafael Correa's Multicolored Dream Shirt: Commerce, Creativity, and National Identity in Post-Neoliberal Ecuador," *Latin American and Caribbean Ethnic Studies* 7, no. 3 (2012): 275–94. Paola Mantilla helped us locate and set up interviews with both Teresa Casa and Alicia Cisneros, played an important role in developing and executing our

2005 survey of Atuntaqui clothing producers, and most recently helped us secure permission to reproduce a number of photos for this book. Aside from being a skilled researcher, Paola was one of Ibarra, Ecuador's smoothest DJs (at Mega 99.9 FM) and is now an increasingly sought-after PR and communications specialist. We are grateful for her participation in this project.

Prologue

Tradition, Innovation, and Artisan Economy in the Northern Andes

His shirt was beautiful. On the eve of taking office in 2007, Ecuadorian President Rafael Correa commissioned a shirt embroidered with Andean symbols from pre-Columbian archaeology (see figure 1a). Debuted at a special inauguration event in the tiny highland town of Zumbagua, the shirt's hand-stitched symbols spoke to the president's promise to promote indigenous communities. The symmetrical stitches on the front panels of the shirt drew on ancient archaeological heritage, inspired by traditional pottery motifs, but blended with artisan innovation and contemporary design. By innovating on an ancient tradition, Correa deliberately broke from another tradition—the business suits and banker attire usually donned by Latin American presidents. Correa linked Ecuador to a resurgent leftward-leaning leadership in Latin America, explicitly allying with Venezuela's Hugo Chávez and Bolivia's Evo Morales, while reaching back to the most prominent breaker of business-suit tradition, Cuba's Fidel Castro.

In 2007, it was most uncertain whether Correa—or his shirt—

would be successful. For two decades, Ecuador had lurched between economic crises and political strife. Since 1996, no Ecuadorian president had lasted more than three years in office. Presidential candidates promised economic sovereignty from global markets, yet once in office they pledged austerity to the International Monetary Fund in exchange for loans. As an ultimate capitulation to global markets, Ecuador declared "dollarization" in 2000, abandoning its devalued national currency for the US dollar. General strikes, military coups, and street protests cut short president after president. Amid the political fiascos, more than one million Ecuadorians emigrated to the United States, Spain, and Italy.

Meanwhile, the neighboring northern country of Colombia had opted for the business-suit tradition. In 2006, Colombians reelected President Álvaro Uribe, whose campaign themes were security, stability, efficiency, and the image of workaholic austerity. Uribe's business suits reflected a technocrat tradition, eschewing the socialist and populist themes from neighboring countries and the new leftward-leaning Latin American leaders (see figure 1b). But beneath the apparent presidential stability, Colombia was home to the longest-running guerrilla conflict in the hemisphere. Uribe promised to confront and defeat the leftist FARC, the Revolutionary Armed Forces of Colombia, after peace negotiations failed in 2002. With large landowners enlisting paramilitary hit squads, people in rural areas were caught between right-wing paramilitary organizations and the FARC guerrillas. Colombia regularly topped international lists for human rights concerns because of the numbers of homicides, internally displaced people, kidnappings, and extortion.

For many Colombians, Correa's election made them feel surrounded by leftist governments in neighboring Venezuela and Ecuador, while still fighting the FARC. The Colombian government played up suspicions of ties between the FARC, Chávez, and Correa. After Colombia's 2008 cross-border raid into Ecuador pursuing FARC guerillas, Ecuador and Venezuela cut off diplomatic ties and moved troops to the border. The tensions

IA)

IB)

FIGURE IA, IB. Presidential styles in the Northern Andes: Rafael Correa of Ecuador, Álvaro Uribe of Colombia, and Secretary of State Hillary Clinton of the United States (Photos: US government)

between Uribe and Correa could not be starker. Like their clothing differences, the two leaders seemed to be treading markedly different paths, epitomizing the extremes of Latin American response to the realignments of economic and political globalization.

After an emergency summit, Chávez, Correa, and Uribe shook

hands and embraced. Tensions eased. But what is truly remarkable is that with all the political strife, and even with the global economic crises and panics of what is now called the Great Recession, this has been a time of relative stability for Ecuador and Colombia. Correa became the longest-running president of Ecuador since the 1970s. His ethnic-themed shirts remained his trademark icon, and he gifted shirts to Hugo Chávez, Evo Morales, and US Secretary of State Hillary Clinton. Uribe likewise became the longest-serving president in Colombia in over a century, and was succeeded by Juan Manuel Santos. Santos had been Uribe's minister of defense and Uribe had anointed him as a successor. Santos and Correa also met in the border city of Tulcán, Ecuador, agreeing on further border integration and greater economic-political cooperation. In June 2014, Santos was reelected to the Colombian presidency in what was seen as a referendum on his negotiations for peace with the FARC.

Indeed, despite the talk of socialism and citizens' revolution from Correa, Ecuador's policy pragmatics rather resemble what Santos calls a Third Way: "use the markets as much as possible and the state as much as necessary" (interview by Tim Padgett in *Time*, April 12, 2012). Perhaps the most potent similarity between the Ecuadorian and Colombian programs is how both emphasize innovation. The Colombian plan names innovation as the first of its "three pillars." Innovation is the first pillar that permeates and stimulates all other fields:

> Innovation is the best mechanism to ensure the sustainability of growth and the country's competitiveness over the long term. Innovation not only means developing new products and transforming existing products. Innovation consists of creating new ways to organize, manage, produce, deliver, market, sell and interact with customers and suppliers; its final achievement is to generate added value through the entire production chain. This is why innovation and investment in research and development are not exclusively for the high-technology sector. On the contrary, it must be a vital part of all economic sectors and extends to all their linkages. (Departamento Nacional de Planeación 2011, 7)[1]

Although the Ecuadorian plan (Movimiento Alianza PAIS 2013) does not include such an extensive discussion, ideas and language of innovation appear many times. Like the Colombian plan, innovation is portrayed as key to developing science, technology, and education, but also as applied to economic productivity and even cultural activities. The Ecuadorian plan emphasizes a rupture from traditional norms and hierarchies. With three exceptions—for traditional knowledge, traditional medicine, and oral tradition—the traditional is almost always used in a pejorative sense, whereas innovation is always phrased positively.[2]

The Andean presidents' focus is a sign of the times. The uncertain profitability of traditional industry, the big earnings of Google, Apple, and other technology-driven businesses, the ubiquitous pressures of global finance, and the threat from upstarts anywhere in the world seem to have put all businesses on notice: earnings today in no way promise earnings tomorrow. "Innovation. It's the lifeblood of our global economy and a strategic priority for virtually every CEO around the world," write business gurus Jeff Dyer, Hal Gregersen, and Clayton Christensen as a blurb for *The Innovator's DNA: Mastering the Five Skills of Disruptive Innovators* (2011).

What is most intriguing in the writings on innovation by these and other authors is less the profiles of hard-driving entrepreneurs such as Steve Jobs or Jeff Bezos. Rather, it is the portrait of innovation that they offer: innovation as cheap, low-brow, half-cocked, intrusive, democratized. Christensen (1997) famously showed that "disruptive technologies"—innovations that result in "worse product performance"—defy the skill and power of well-run, established firms. Low-margin, low-performing new goods set in motion changes that result in big profits and wide new markets. Eric von Hippel (2005) shows that the tinkering of users challenges designing by manufacturers when it comes to creative new products. He argues that innovation is becoming democratized, creating communities that link up makers and users and sustaining a commons, a shared public domain of information and intellectual exchange.

Our research also centers on innovation and disruption. Our research area is the very northern Andean heartland where Correa first journeyed in search of a presidential shirt and where conflicts between Ecuador and Colombia play out in the commerce of ordinary citizens. Here there is a ceaseless supply of disruptive, open-access, interactive innovation, with relentless focus on being cheaper, smaller, and convenient. In this region dominated by artisan craft production, family firms, and peasant market plazas, we wanted to know how artisans innovate, earn from their creativity, and relate innovations to traditional identities. Internationally, the region is famous for an indigenous-ethnic clothing trade centered in Otavalo, Ecuador, where many of the products sold as indigenous are really relatively recent inventions. Artisans may innovate, but in an economy of market display and competition, innovations can be quickly copied. Distant competitors can appropriate designs or displace local sales. A neighbor can rush out replicas of a product that has started to sell well. To bring the matter back to the president: What is the value of artisan *innovation*—or indeed, the meaning of artisan *tradition*—when within weeks of Correa's inauguration there were $7 semimechanized knockoffs of the presidential shirt for sale in Otavalo's Indian Market?

The Northern Andes, Capitalism, and the Globalized Artisan

What we call the northern Andean highlands is an area of mountainous settlements and provincial cities stretching from a southern range of Ambato, Ecuador, to a northern expanse of Pasto, Colombia, with Ecuador's capital city of Quito as the regional epicenter (see figure 2). In relation to the classic central Andean heartland of contemporary Peru and Bolivia, the home of the Inca Empire, this is the far end of the northern Andes, a region of ancient and powerful chiefdoms. The late Inca Empire eventually incorporated some of this region, but the people in the northern fringe successfully resisted Inca advances—events in this area would lead to a civil war for succession, leaving the Inca

FIGURE 2. Colombia, Ecuador, and the research communities (Map credit: Amanda Clark Henley, used by permission)

Empire vulnerable as Francisco Pizarro's expedition was able to rally indigenous allies (Cahill 2010). But despite this fragmentation, there are some shared regional features of language, clothing, and cuisine, such as cuy, the domesticated guinea pig prized throughout the Andean highlands.

This area straddles the equator, so there is little seasonal variation. Days and nights are of equal duration throughout the year. Vegetation and crops depend on the dramatic microclimate variation resulting from altitude changes—a day's journey on foot can traverse cold-climate potatoes, through corn and wheat, then to hot-climate cotton and sugarcane. These are mountain settlements, but the coastal areas and the Amazon region are geographically close and interlinked. Going further north in Colombia, the Andes begin to split into three distinct mountain ranges, and the Colombian coast, mountain, and Amazonian rain forest are not so closely linked. And people in the north of the country do not eat cuy.

This region of our study is a northern extension of a classic Andean pattern. For the most part farming is done in small plots, at the household level. Female market vendors sell produce in colorful peasant markets (see figure 3a, b, c). The region is rife with artisan goods, most famously knit sweaters and woven ponchos; but there are also woven belts, tailored shirts and pants, sandals and hats, leatherwork, woodwork, jewelry, and paintings. Like many tourists and anthropologists, Correa chose an obvious path when he came here to seek something authentically Ecuadorian. This is the bedrock of Andean artisan tradition, and this area is typically portrayed as opposed to innovation, with inhabitants locked into old ways and routine. The people are assumed to be either those who conserve traditional highland indigenous customs, like the Otavalos, or are *mestizo* peasants, Spanish-speaking rural folk who are attached to the land and agrarian life.

Of course in Otavalo today, fast-food vendors dole out hamburgers and pizza, everyone has a cell phone, there are plenty of places renting Internet terminals, and stores sell electronics

3A)

3B)

3C)

FIGURE 3A, 3B, 3C. Highland provincial peasant markets: Túquerres, Colombia (2009); Otavalo, Ecuador (2009); Zumbagua, Ecuador (2013) (Photos: a. Jason Antrosio; b. and c. Rudi Colloredo-Mansfeld)

and factory-woven blankets imported from Asia. A discerning artisan-ware shopper can spot the Peruvian crafts now sold alongside Otavalo market stands. There are T-shirt factories and a booming casual fashion industry in Atuntaqui, just north of Otavalo. It would be quite tempting to conclude that this is a traditional region about to be swept into capitalist globalization, that the products of traditional artisans are about to be displaced, that they will soon all be working in factories or riding buses to work on enormous cut-flower operations, or swelling the ranks of the urban poor.

It is a tempting story, but it is not a true one. The true story of the northern Andes is surprising. First, there was a great deal of international activity in this region during the early years of the twentieth century, especially from the turn of the century until the 1930s. Spanish investors built one of the largest textile factories in South America in Atuntaqui, importing machinery and managers from Europe and the United States. Large landholders and merchants established import-export operations and opened international connections between the highlands and the coast. Then, in the 1950s–1970s, Otavalo weavers and marketers innovated with international patterns for tourist sales, Atuntaqui factory laborers used their knowledge and earnings to establish home-based production, and small farmers in northern Ecuador and southwestern Colombia used new hybrid potato varieties to out-compete the larger haciendas. In short, every part of the pattern currently perceived as traditional was intertwined with capitalist innovations and global transformations.

Correa's presidential shirt is a good example. The shirt is an odd fit for socialist rhetoric or even as an emblem of an ancient nation. Its iconic design elements—simple collar, puffy sleeves, and hand embroidery—are mixed up with hippie entrepreneurs, American marketers, design piracy, Hollywood films of piracy, indigenous capitalists, and the hard bargaining of open-air markets. Put bluntly, Correa's shirt represents a deep capitalist habit, and has become the latest link in a long chain of knockoffs. Most immediately it reflects the style of goods sold as Otavalo wedding shirts in the famous Otavalo craft market. This shirt in turn seems to have developed from garments that were based on a local, pleated dress shirt known as the *tiu camisa* (Meisch 2002), which Peace Corps volunteers in the early 1970s had helped indigenous entrepreneurs redesign and sell to a new flow of budget travelers through Otavalo.

For forty years, people have sized up this garment and convinced themselves that they could work it for a profit. Over the years, seamstresses in Otavalo and Ibarra, embroiders in Zuleta, and a US-based catalog retailer, the J. Peterman Company, sold variations of this shirt. The puffy shirt commerce connected rural places with provincial cities. Mestizos partnered with US entrepreneurs to mass produce an indigenous product; indigenous artisans adopted computerized embroidering machines to supply export markets in Chile and Brazil. While the shirt's identity has melded with Otavalo, men and women in other towns have blazed parallel paths of designing and deal making. In fact, we head north from Otavalo to Ibarra to present that city's updating of the *tiu camisa*. There, production cross-linked Ibarra and US pop culture in startling ways. In Ibarra, too, an artisan stepped up with a precise and practiced hand to embroider President Correa's shirt when others were unable. A helpful place to begin this version of the story is with one small detail that helped launch the shirt's career: the zigzag line.

Zigzags, Hippie Piracy, and Hollywood Pirates: Otavalo Shirt v1.0

Dolores Quinche's father had moved to the bustling regional city of Ibarra from the indigenous village of Quinchuqui. Years later, during an interview in July 2011 on a shaded porch at the edge of her patio, Dolores explained what she knew of the history of the Otavalo wedding shirt. "The shirts that my father wore, for example, they call 'pleated shirts,'" Dolores explained. "They were a model worn especially by those from Quinchuqui and Natabuela also." Dolores was a younger cousin of Hermelina Males, the woman many in Ibarra credit with designing and producing the first commercial version of the wedding shirt. Dolores and Hermelina had lived near each other in the provincial capital. Hermelina had died years before and Dolores was one of the few left who had known her well.

The lives of Hermelina and her cousin Dolores had converged in significant ways. There was the brief medical course they participated in, the first indigenous women in Ibarra to receive such training. Then there was their choice of spouses. Not only had each married a Frenchman, but these men had novel occupations amid their contemporaries. Hermelina's spouse was a musicologist, Dolores's an organic farmer. Their international matches were one sign of the surprisingly cosmopolitan world that the northern Andes had become. In the early 1970s, the children of rural migrants to the city pushed indigenous expressive arts in new directions and found allies in traveling foreigners. Venues in Ibarra featured skilled musicians performing traditional Andean music. Indigenous women, including Dolores, came together to found a dance group called Muyacan that integrated forgotten details of traditional women's clothing styles into the choreography. Working with artistic directors from Ecuador and Chile, they performed internationally.

"Yes, my father wore these pleated shirts, embroidered in the cuffs and the collar, but *quingiado* (zigzagged), like this." Dolores reached down and traced her finger along the hem of her long skirt where a single thread tightly tacked back and forth (see figure 4). "This is the *quingu.*" Dolores then broke off the interview and went in search of her husband's wedding shirt. When she returned, she continued to explain about the meaning of zigzagging:

> But *quingiado* can indicate a lot of things. When one talks up too directly, too abruptly in Quichua, another says "speak with discretion and elegance—*Quingushpa rimaychi.*" One might say, "go with elegance, slowly and with moderation—*Quingushpa richi*" one would want to say. Quingu one finds on the road, "*Quingushpa purichi*— walk smoothly and in peace."

FIGURE 4. Embroidery detail from an original Otavalo wedding shirt, c. 1975 (Photo: Rudi Colloredo-Mansfeld)

As Dolores talked, she gave the sense of an aesthetic of subtle moves. But to some extent, this was only natural. An indigenous woman who had grown up among artisans and musicians and who had performed in a nationally known dance group, Dolores had found a word to conjure a sense of elegance, urbanity, and indigenousness. Dolores's father had been a pioneer of indigenous city life, an early migrant from the peasant farming community of Quinchuqui to Ibarra. To sit with Dolores in a house in the middle of urban Ibarra and hear Quichua, Spanish, and French spoken among three generations is to be reminded that indigenous lives could zigzag between country and city, the northern Andes and far-flung locales.

In this milieu, Hermelina and her husband developed their design for the wedding shirt. Hermelina preserved the traditional pleated front, but she embellished the embroidery beyond the simple zigzag. Hermelina's shirts featured diamonds filled with cross-hatches of colored thread and bordered by thin, arc-ing lines crossing each other in delicate patterns. Musicians and dancers in Ibarra drove demand for the shirts. The shirts could also be marketed to the growing number of North American and European backpackers traveling the "gringo trail," an itinerary of ruins, natural wonders, and indigenous cultures running through South America. These backpackers demonstrated a potential early market for handicrafts, a growing selection of products such as wall hangings and sweaters that put traditional skills to new use.

Perhaps most importantly, in the flow of adventurers, backpackers, hippies, mountain climbers, and searchers were also the entrepreneurs. Some of those free-spirited hippies glimpsed profit from artisan handicraft quality, low-cost labor, and favorable exchange rates. To keep up with demand, Hermelina contracted with a seamstress in Ibarra nicknamed La Lojanita, a mestiza who had a successful tailoring business. Within a few years they had clients in the United States and Canada. Two clients with the same name began buying the wedding shirts with such regularity that Hermelina and La Lojanita took to calling the shirt *Camisa John.*

Hermelina died from a botched cesarean. The memory of the shoddy medical treatment still brings anger to Dolores's voice, forty years later. To this day, it keeps her fighting for respect for indigenous women in Ibarra. Dolores also noted that Hermelina's death is why she knows little of the history of the shirt since the days when her husband acquired his wedding shirt from her cousin. Hermelina and her husband had been Dolores's contact with the shirt trade. Although Hermelina's daughter had lived, her father took her with him to France. For a number of years he continued to pass orders to La Lojanita. But their relationship grew strained as he left the artisan scene in Ibarra, and La Lojanita went in search of her own clients at expensive Quito craft galleries.

We interviewed La Lojanita and two of her sons who still work with her in the business in July 2009. She explained to us that some of her original foreign clients stuck with her. More placed orders and then her sons joined in the business. In the 1980s, their operation grew to sixty employees, with an additional 120 women subcontracted as embroiderers. They had close partnerships with US firms and one of her clients relocated to Ibarra to work more closely with the company. He spent almost two years living with the family and managing sales.

The gringo turned out to be an ungrateful guest. When he moved out, he took with him many of La Lojanita's new clients, and he began supplying them shirts from a new manufacturing operation he had been setting up on the side. Around this time, US catalogs began selling versions of the shirt. Most prominently, the J. Peterman Company promoted what they called the Otavalo Mountain Shirt. This item would be among their regular goods, and as of 2014, the text on the J. Peterman Company website continued to promote the shirt: "It's the real thing: the actual cotton workshirt actually worn by the actual mountain people of Otavalo, Ecuador. For about the past four centuries." The words drive home a timeless, authentic tradition—real, actual, actually, actual, four centuries. In reality, of course, the shirt is not timeless but very much of its time. As Lynn Meisch reveals, it is a design that, at most, goes back 150 years, is hardly worn by anyone in Otavalo today, and has been fine-tuned among high volume Ibarra producers (2002, 99).[3]

As the US firms took over the stories and the branding, La Lojanita's family lost sales and employees. To rebuild, they signed up for trade shows during New York Fashion Week and a Western wear apparel show in Las Vegas. In some ways, the business reversals and renewals had preserved Hermelina's garment relatively intact. It was still tailored from heavy cotton fabric, pleated and with a simple band, or "mandarin," collar. The company continued to use sewing machines acquired decades earlier. Rather than streamlining production with computers and plotters that optimize the layout of pieces on the fabric for cutting, they had a modest cutting table and laid out patterns by hand. Bolts of cloth had to be carefully tracked and pieces matched so that items shrunk uniformly. While seamstresses in Atuntaqui's

FIGURE 5. Between artisanship and industry: making the Otavalo wedding shirt, Ibarra, 2009 (Photo: Rudi Colloredo-Mansfeld)

home-based casual apparel shops had learned to assemble simple T-shirts in less than two minutes, in La Lojanita's plant a machine operator took thirty to thirty-five minutes to sew together the pieces of the Otavalo wedding shirt (see figure 5). If La Lojanita's operation seemed larger than artisanal, it stopped short of being industrial.

The most significant change since the time of Hermelina was the source of the raw material. In the 2000s, the family imported everything from the United States. With 100 percent US cotton, their clothes qualified for favorable import duties on return shipment. As a dedicated exporter, the company had become largely invisible to residents of its home city.

Then in 2003, the family starred in its own Hollywood story. Their shirts were chosen to clad the extras in the Johnnie Depp film *Pirates of the Caribbean: The Curse of the Black Pearl*. A costume designer had seen la Lojanita's "renaissance" line exhibited at the Western wear show in Las Vegas. At first, the producers had talked about four thousand shirts for all the extras. In the end, the film's producers purchased 150, a small sale but one that brought a lot of attention. It turned out that the step from Andean artisan to pop culture stardom could at times be small.

For a business that was born amid an economy of backpackers, organic farming and Andean music, the trade in Otavalo wedding shirts has been a successful lesson in competitive survival in a global economy. La Lojanita and her children developed the possibilities of their market niche, becoming purveyors of rustic, exotic, and nostalgic clothes. The fringes of North American culture have a soft spot for puffy sleeves; this small Ecuadorian producer took care of it. The global capitalism that shaped the economic landscape around Ibarra in the early twentieth century had its counterpart in the intimate internationalism of this venture. A three-way cultural collaboration—indigenous, mestizo, and French—supplied a fourth cultural yearning in North America. And yet, through four decades of exports and a growing array of business partners, the original producer of the Otavalo wedding shirt remained a conservative operation. The seamstress that went to work with Hermelina Males all those years ago, La Lojanita, lived next door to her factory and her employees were still versed in making versions of Hermelina's shirt. Strikingly, it was the indigenous manufacturers and merchants of Otavalo who truly widened the product lines and markets for the Otavalo shirt.

Indian Markets and Machine-Made Artisans: Otavalo Shirt v2.0

In some ways, the first story of the Otavalo shirt seems ripped from a Handbook of Dirty Capitalist Tricks: Step 1, urban indigenous elites commercialize traditional indigenous design; Step 2, national entrepreneurs further co-opt indigenous design; Step 3, multinational corporations make off with the brand; Step 4, they never look back. It is a story heard the world over, although the *Pirates of the Caribbean* gives this one a happier twist. What is unusual about the second story of the Otavalo shirt, the story that brings the shirt even greater fame and commercial success, is that it was largely run by indigenous manufacturers and merchants.

On the southern slopes of Mount Imbabura, Dolores's father's home village of Quinchuqui is today at the center of a multimillion-dollar indigenous craft economy. Rural artisan textile producers built the now famous Plaza de Ponchos, or Indian Market, in Otavalo. The Plaza de Ponchos fed off the same "gringo trail" energy that brought backpackers through Ecuador, except this time it was indigenous people trying to figure out how to sell items to tourists. Many of these products could hardly be considered traditional—some had been reverse engineered as knockoffs of popular Scottish tweed items from the 1920s, other sweater designs were taken from the US Peace Corps in the 1960s, and the Plaza de Ponchos itself received Dutch backing for a 1970s redesign.

Otavalo is a startling break from other indigenous artisan stories. Craft economies in Latin America often arise as a kind of layered ethnic exploitation (van den Berghe 1993). Wealthy whites from abroad stay at hotels and buy from shops run by a mestizo middle class who get their goods or labor cheap from indigenous people—what nearly happened in the first story of the Otavalo shirt. In contrast, Otavalo's indigenous people have built hotels, set up air freight companies, and run businesses as aggregators filling shipping containers with sweaters and bags and exporting them to family members who resell them throughout Europe and the Americas. Somewhat ironically, the Otavalo indigenous merchants are often the ones subcontracting sweater knitting to rural mestizo households in a wide network of northern Andean villages.

Yet for all the power that the Plaza de Ponchos provides for Otavalo's indigenous people, the day to day business in the Indian Market can be debilitating. Indeed, one of the unexpected pressures of making a living in an economy of indigenous goods and traditional crafts is the need to constantly innovate. Cotton shirt makers were established in the plaza in the early 1970s, primarily selling unadorned pleated men's shirts in a few basic colors. In subsequent decades, ideas crossed over from other crafts. One producer used the striped cloth woven for lightweight hammocks as raw material. Another began to adorn the front of his shirts with pieces of Inca-themed tablecloths. Jewelers in the market had been experimenting with tagua, a tropical nut that had been promoted as an ivory substitute. Working with tagua vendors, shirt makers tried buttons and beads as details for their shirts. Producers began to contract with embroiderers from communities in Zuleta, an hour's drive away on the northeast side of Mount Imbabura, sending out large quantities of shirts for decoration with flowers and other simple motifs.

By 2005, scores of cotton shirt makers were at work, producing garments that had their origin in the Otavalo wedding shirt. One of the producers had grown to employ fifty machine operators making shirts, pants, and other items. Having outgrown a market stall in the plaza, his family operated a big, modern store with display windows and efficient shelving units stacked with bundles of products for bulk sales. Producers complained about copying, disloyal competition, shoddy workmanship, and a market saturated by overproduction, but the trade was growing.

As president-elect, Rafael Correa also complained about the Plaza de Ponchos. In this case, the innovation seemed too much like crass capitalism—Correa wanted something that he saw as more indigenous, authentic, autochthonous. Correa commissioned a special design team to innovate the traditional. But despite the efforts of at least one of the designers to establish exclusive control, presidential shirt knockoffs would soon be back in the Plaza de Ponchos, interspersed with sweaters, wall hangings, hammocks, embroidered shirts, paintings, pan pipes, tablecloths, chess sets, hats, T-shirts, dream catchers, Plains Indian war bonnets, Panamanian Molas, Peruvian rugs, Bolivian wallets, ceramic incense holders, tagua nut jewelry, and pirated CDs of Andean music. It is a sometimes jarring juxtaposition, yet typical of the northern Andes and beyond. The market combines artisanship and capitalism, simultaneously localizing and globalizing, a constant interlocking of innovation and tradition.

Anthropology of Capitalist Artisans and Globalized Wedding Shirts

Although popular images of anthropology still depict a quest for the pristine traditional and the primitive isolate, anthropologists have long shown that all peoples and cultural traditions are products of interaction and exchange. We both began our anthropological fieldwork with a desire to document people enmeshed in the global economy. We were in the northern Andes, but tackling the problem in different ways. Rudi went to Otavalo, precisely because Otavalo was seen as the setting for the new globetrotting indigenous. Jason went to Túquerres, Colombia, in part because it had completely fallen off the gringo trail—the people there were seen as not-ethnic-at-all, rural agriculturists left behind by a global economy. Interestingly, our initial stints of immersive anthropological fieldwork revealed an overlap in the idea of the modern-traditional symbiosis: how people were using products considered modern, like TVs, stereos, and gas-cooking ranges precisely to bolster activities considered traditional, like artisan weaving and peasant agriculture.

The economic and political crises of Ecuador and Colombia in the early 2000s would bring us together for a joint project in northern Ecuador. In Otavalo, the fiscal reforms that accompanied dollarization badly ruptured the costs, currencies, and supplier relationships. Wide segments of the market chaotically shut down during wool boycotts and rampant inflation. Teenagers in the Otavalo countryside who had learned the skills of production or built inventories of handicrafts to launch their own careers quit the handicraft trade. Some went to work on commercial flower plantations, others emigrated to labor in Spain or Italy, and still others headed to Guayaquil or Bogotá to sell Chinese-made key chains to drivers at stop lights. In Colombia, more and more landowners enlisted paramilitary groups in an effort to oust the guerrillas. For Túquerres, what had been a place of relative calm and tranquility became a place of danger and death squads. As anthropologists, we had to reconsider what we had been studying and begin thinking of new projects.

In the midst of economic and political turmoil, there were nevertheless growing trades. One was the Otavalo shirt makers. Another was in neighboring Atuntaqui, experiencing a boom in home-based manufacturing for casual-wear clothing. We wanted to know what accounted for these successes during the ravages of economic dislocation and global competition. Two lines of inquiry oriented our work. First, what value did cultural identity have in sustaining cooperation among rivals within a community trade? Second, we wanted to understand the fate of ideas and innovations in artisan marketplaces with no intellectual property protections. How do communities both exploit and regenerate the shared ideas that give value to their commodities? We framed the core of our project as a variant of a commons problem, the challenge that a group faces when living from a shared resource. In these trades and marketplaces, the shared resources were not pastures or forests but rather hereditary artisan designs, shared professional reputations for manufacturing skill, and the jointly used market plazas, business districts, and annual events that attracted visitors.

As conditions stabilized, we have been able to revisit people in Colombia and Ecuador who had been displaced by crises, helping to place the Atuntaqui-Otavalo comparison within a larger northern Andean context. The unexpected emphasis and convergence on the idea of innovation by both the Ecuadorian and Colombian governments—countries that once seemed on such divergent paths—widen the implications of our research to national development. Finally, when all this time we have been working on local agriculture, artisan manufacture, and family economy in Latin America, the idea of the artisan, local food, and local economy has newly come into fashion. Studying actual artisans in the Andes, we returned to find that artisans were now trendy in the United States.

The Artisan Returns: Invasive Trades, Invaded Communities

Artisans are back. The crusty bread, the craft cheese with locally pickled cornichons, the handmade sandals and handspun cloth. They speak to us of the traditional and yet are the newly desired must-haves. Unexpectedly, artisans spin dreams of individual and collective economic revival. *New York Times* columnist Thomas Friedman, once the biggest shill for the benefits of globalization, now regularly trumpets artisan values as a solution for struggling workers:

> I think Lawrence Katz, the Harvard University labor economist, has it right. Everyone today, he says, needs to think of himself as an "artisan"—the term used before mass manufacturing to apply to people who made things or provided services with a distinctive touch in which they took personal pride. Everyone today has to be an artisan and bring something extra to their jobs. (October 23, 2010)

Friedman insists that being an artisan, bringing that something extra to the job, is the only way for individual workers to escape an economy dominated by "McWages." As global economic competition turns out to have more pernicious outcomes than the previously promised prosperity, advice to "think like an artisan" offers a way out (Friedman and Mandelbaum 2011, 137).[1]

This uplifting theme runs through many accounts positing how artisans and a local economy can solve the woes of industrial capitalism and globalization. Embracing artisan values represents the next stage of capitalism while recapturing its true spirit. Adam Davidson, Friedman's colleague at the *New York Times* describes a change in fortunes for the economy, not just individual workers. In an article titled online as "Don't Mock the Artisanal-Pickle Makers," Davidson says: "It's tempting to look at craft businesses as simply a rejection of modern industrial capitalism. But the craft approach is actually something new—a happy refinement of the excesses of our industrial era plus a return to the vision laid out by capitalism's godfather, Adam Smith" (February 15, 2012).

Similarly, Michael Shuman's vision of *The Small-Mart Revolution: How Local Businesses Are Beating the Global Competition* (2006) tells of how mom-and-pop stores, farmers' markets, local food producers, hometown banks, small-scale manufacturers, and downtown merchant alliances could consolidate into a self-sustaining economy of work and wealth. Shuman takes this idea further in *Local Dollars, Local Sense: How to Shift Your Money from Wall Street to Main Street and Achieve Real Prosperity* (2012), imagining local investment clubs and local stock exchanges. Apparently local livestock for the farmers' market is not enough—we need our own local stock markets.

Somewhat curiously, the artisan has also appeared as the hero of a very different story: the artisan as anticapitalism and antimarket. In this account, the artisan embodies a precapitalist ethos, nearly desolated by the likes of Adam Smith and his ilk, but now revived in an effort to move beyond, away, or outside of capitalism. Richard Sennett's work *The Craftsman* (2008) and his follow-up, *Together: The Rituals, Pleasures and Politics of Cooperation* (2012), posit craft and cooperation as fundamental but threatened aspects of human nature.

Here, artisans become alternatives to capitalism. Artisans produce for fundamentally nonmarket needs, for family and com-

munity, under constant threat of market and capitalist encroach-
ment. These ideas often invoke not just a local economy but a
commons, a nonmarket, community-based resource everywhere
threatened by global capitalism. J. K. Gibson-Graham's work on
A Postcapitalist Politics makes this most explicit: "the commons
can be seen as a community stock that needs to be maintained
and replenished so that it can continue to constitute the community by providing its direct input (subsidy) to survival" (2006, 97).

These are paradoxical positions from artisan partisans—how
can the artisan and the local economy be both at the vanguard
of capitalism and the vanguard of anticapitalism? This paradox
parallels the apparent contradiction discussed in the prologue,
how the ostensibly procapitalist government of Colombia and
the ostensibly revolutionary government of Ecuador both emphasize policies of innovation, as contrasted to tradition.

Part of the paradox can be resolved by stepping away from
the typical simplifications and ideal-type visions of capitalism
that are often used by pundits and analysts. These commentators have a knack for turning people who are actually growing
vegetables, making cheese, or knitting sweaters into abstractions.
When we turn to the more mundane realities of people crafting
things, together, we discover a different perspective from those
who would enlist artisans for either the capitalist or the postcapitalist cause. We find neither blind adherence to tradition nor
constant innovation, but people who must perpetually adjust and
work skillfully with materials. In short, the turn to anthropological analysis and ethnographic fieldwork helps to dislodge some
of these persistent dichotomies.

However, anthropological fieldwork and ethnography by
themselves are not a cure-all for this kind of dichotomous thinking. This is because anthropology inherited a long history of
looking at the world through categories imported from a powerful vision formed during the rise of industrial capitalism. These
categories seemed to describe human economy and natural ecology, but were in fact visions of how that economy and ecology
should be. These categories did not just describe the world, they

contained a prescription for it. They were rooted in a particular experience in northern Europe, but they were exported as truths for all people, as universal models for economy and ecology (Trouillot 2003, 35–38).

These ideas revolved around notions that both human economies and natural ecologies have natural end points—they are in unidirectional motion from one state to the next. Moreover, the means of that unidirectional motion is a mechanism: a market mechanism that uses competition to produce efficient activity in the economy and a natural selection mechanism that uses competition to produce efficient creatures in the ecosystem.[2] These two ideas were linked and used interchangeably, becoming powerful templates for seeing the world. In this vision, artisans were everywhere in a competition that would drive them out of their workshops and into agglomeration and efficient capitalist-industrial organization. Ecological resources like commons land and fisheries would inevitably be degraded because of individualized competition. It was always the Tragedy of the Commons, or differently put, the Triumph of Capitalism. As is still often the case, political positions intersected with description—the artisan and the commons were always part of a disappearing past, a past perhaps to be cherished or mourned, or perhaps even to be celebrated and renewed, or a past to be forgotten, despised, and superseded. But always in the past or somewhere else, similar to visitors to the northern Andes today who may see themselves as stepping out of contemporary time and into another, more traditional time.

It takes some rather dramatic rethinking to see ongoing symbiosis between artisan and capitalist forms. It can be difficult to recover the many instances in which commons resources can be quite well-managed over long periods of time, or to understand how a commons resource can emerge from market activities. Similarly, new and more dynamic approaches have emerged in ecology, which view organisms as always interconnected and with a variety of possible emergent outcomes. Ecological systems are always in transformation, which has led to development of new frameworks for understanding invasive species in a larger ecosystem. Taking a cue from earlier borrowings of metaphor and meaning between ecology and economy, we see artisan activities as often emerging from an invasive trade with wider effects on the community.

Our project involves rethinking these templates regarding the directionality and mechanisms of economic change. We put these templates to the test of ethnographic evidence, both from our own work in the northern Andes, but also by reading anthropological and other accounts. This is what we have found:

1. *Artisans live with a great deal of risk, uncertainty, and often work in winner-take-all economies.* Whereas artisan life is imagined to be a stable, predictable routine, we find people involved in risky ventures. Uncertain outcomes result in a winner-take-all distribution. In fact, the lure of a big windfall, a winner-take-all payout, can be the sustaining motivation to continue manual artisan labor.

2. *Artisans are thoroughly intertwined with capitalism.* Unlike those who see artisans as embodying a new phase of capitalism—or as a pre-, post-, or anticapitalist alternative—artisan work has always been at the heart of the capitalist system. Artisans have provided unacknowledged inputs for industrial capitalism. Artisan activities have reemerged in the heart of industry. And artisans often are the result of industry as much as they are a precursor to it.

3. *Artisans are always entangled in legal definitions and state regulations.* Artisans do not exist outside of state regulation, nor do they preexist an advancing state government. Rather, artisans have always been involved in struggles over regulations and who should legally count as part of the artisan economy. State governance and legal definitions can generate artisan activities as much as they regulate the sector.

4. *Artisan activities can stem from invasive trades, adding an additional element to a historically invaded community.* Although capitalism and globalization can certainly be destabilizing forces, artisan economies often enter and thrive as a consequence of destabilization. Artisan activities can be invasive, as a productive practice spreads rapidly in places that have been unsettled or degraded. However, these invasive activities can then be regularized and routinized,

transforming into a new tradition or creating a new commons. In these historically invaded communities, an invasive trade can be transformed into a new community resource.

Invasion Ecology, Invaded Economies

As family after family goes into the same type of new business, what initially might have seemed like economic growth or boom can feel more like a takeover. All around, the same goods spread out for sale; older businesses disappear under a blanket of similar new commodities. A town experiences an insurgent moment, the virulent replication of a market-ready product. Inspired by descriptions from the field of invasion ecology, we name this an invasive trade. In the natural world, such invasions often come about with the arrival of organisms through human activity to areas outside their native range (Elton 1958). These situations, though, are rarely simple. The introductions can involve patterns of florescence, rapid evolution, and competition with native species, hyper and tenacious development, disequilibrium, and system change (Richardson 2011; Rotherham and Lambert 2011). For example, offspring of the goats that settlers brought to the Galapagos Islands went feral, thrived, spread, and stripped a number of islands of vegetation. Unable to compete, many of the islands' famed tortoises were pushed out of their native habitat and were at risk of starvation. Conservationists hired sharpshooters, released sterilized female "Judas goats" to lure out the reclusive males, and flew aerial patrols to aid eradication. Then the successful killing of the goats had an unintended consequence: not only did native plant species make a comeback, but the population of human-introduced blackberry bushes took off as the goats no longer held the plant in check.

The field of invasion ecology has unveiled many such surprises. Biologists have tracked these secondary invasions and the complex ways that native and new species interact, discovering interesting paradoxes. To offer one example, at small scales, greater numbers of native species in the affected ecosystem mean less acceptance of invaders, while the fewer the species, the wider the invasion. But at larger scales, the effect reverses: more native species allows more acceptance of invasive species (Richardson, Pyšek, and Carlton 2011). Drawing on such examples from invasion ecology, we are particularly interested in places with long histories of introductions and invasions, the "historically invaded community" (Heard, Sax, and Bruno 2012; Bruno et al. 2004).

For this book, raising the idea of invasive trades and historically invaded communities usefully draws attention to key elements in these artisan stories—novelty, rapid dispersion, the loss of prior trades, rapid systemic change, degradation or growth. A comparison to invasion biology focuses the discussion on how a commodity spreads rapidly in economies that have been unsettled or degraded through urbanization, out-migration, or the collapse of a once fruitful occupation. Peasant communities, old factory towns, and provincial market centers have all been buffeted by new forms of global exchange. But the tireless drive for new markets in the global economy also sets up such locations as the new frontier for entrepreneurs, development specialists, and speculators. Some are merchants contracting with cheap suppliers; others are government technicians offering training and strategies. Thus, even when trades are homegrown, local innovations are borne on the backs of imported technology, international business partners, or a novel kind of external patronage, whether a deep-pockets collector, a visionary retailer, or an ambitious state functionary.

Invasive trades are not to be confused with fads, which are sudden mass markets for fashionable items that go as quickly as they come. The invasive trades and goods involved may be novelties but they are also transformational: they change the character, condition, and possibilities of the places involved. Brash new kinds of economic behaviors drive this change, including winner-take-all competition, speculative over-investment, and rapid reproduction of designs. Consequently, these economies can produce steep inequalities, entail a lot of risk, and crowd out traditional work and products. Under certain circumstances, they come to grief in an invasive meltdown, with markets burning out even as more families flock to the trade for a chance at the payoffs.

Anthropologists and rural sociologists have long had their eye on jarring change that comes with the spread of the world economy. Reviewing the history of the rural upheavals and peasant wars of the twentieth century, anthropologist Eric Wolf wrote of the way that "capitalism cut through the integument of custom, severing people from their accustomed social matrix" (1969, 279). After years of research on land reform and rural development in Latin America, sociologist Alain de Janvry concluded that "the growth of capitalist relations in the periphery feeds upon the stagnation, impoverishment and destruction of the peasant and artisan" (1981, 22). In the Ecuadorian Andes, anthropologist Mary Weismantel (1988) saw not so much the elimination of one economy by another but the literal unhappy marriage of the two. In the early 1980s, husbands from the parish of Zumbagua left to work construction and other jobs in Quito while wives took on more responsibility for farming. "The formation of a household made up of a proletarian male and subsistence farmer female may drive individuals apart in their political and ideological practice, but ultimately semiproletarianization does not so much divide households as unite economies, interlocking rural and capitalist sectors so as to permit the transfer of value from one to the other" (Weismantel 1988, 31–32).

The idea of an invasive economics reengages these issues. However, by attending closely to the details of local enterprises, commodity designs, and market practice, we look at the way invasive trades provoke their own countermovement. There is not so much a backlash against foreign practices, but rather a rapid evolution. Local response channels and begins to regulate disruptive practices. What was once peculiar, and uniquely profitable, can emerge as a more mundane community tradition. The settings and habits of a new trade become regularized as an economic patrimony. The risky new market niche becomes a heritage to be protected and handed down. In these recombinant economies, the novel and alien actually create openings for the collective: an invasive trade becomes a new resource for the historically invaded community.

Here, the arc of the story of contemporary Latin American artisans bends back toward that of the US artisans discussed at the outset, those who are building alternative economies and community through their handcrafted goods. Across these artisan histories, there is the pull of shared economic life. In some writings, the image of the old English commons has been revived and used to explain the spirit and politics of the joint economic base (Gudeman 2005). Staking a strong position, some insist that the commons are "the substantive grounds for collective life" (Reid and Taylor 2010, 12). The politics of the commons becomes no less than a global justice movement. This view pits the sharing, reciprocity, and stewardship of the commons against the self-interest of the market and warns of public domains being lost to private profit (Gudeman 2001; Nonini 2007). While a lofty ideal, this sentiment speaks to some of the grittiest struggles, involving the insistence on the right to ply a trade and to challenge a municipal government to allow peddling of artisan wares in the street.

For others, the commons means community governance of natural resources whose very nature has historically made them difficult to privatize—migrating fish stocks and highland pastures. In his famous 1968 essay "The Tragedy of the Commons," Garrett Hardin insisted rational individuals would never live on shared resources in a sustainable way. In response, many scholars have shown how communities, in fact, often avoided tragedy and successfully managed fisheries, grazing lands, and forests (Acheson 1988; Agrawal 2003; McCay and Acheson 1987; Ostrom et al. 2002). This extensive literature on community use of resources has offered an outline that is now extended beyond natural resource extraction to the world of ideas and the future of cultural commons (Hyde 2010; Lessig 2001, 2004).

What matters in these cases of rapidly changing artisan economies is the way cultural commons emerge in crowded and fiercely competitive trades. Neither a vestige of prior, noncapitalist relations, nor an alternative economic sphere, the commons brings out artisans as a public economy. The inescapable facts of the shared value of their commodities, of their blended reputations, and of the literal common ground of their stores ensure a mutuality that is part and parcel of their rivalry. This interdependence can most keenly be felt when betrayed—in a moment of "disloyal competition" as it is known in Andean market plazas—when product pricing, shoddiness, or copying threatens the future of others.

As previously noted, Gibson-Graham has insisted on the necessity of caring for such shared economic foundations as a commons and community stock (2006, 97). And yet, Gibson-Graham turns away from market relations to go in search of this commons. More than that, this analysis revels in pushing the market aside and stripping from capitalism any of its humanity: "We have installed a naked and visible monster in [capitalism's] place" (1996, 263). But for an artisan whose day job is producing commodities and selling them for a profit, this naked monster makes a raw companion. Many artisans know full well how markets can move to brutal destructiveness. Rather than strip market relations bare, they debate and defend what they owe each other in the practice of their trade, what it would take so that those who follow can find a productive career there. To understand all this requires not looking away from commercial lives and the habits of the market, but observing closely the social connections and cultural stakes at work there.

Perhaps most intriguingly, the social relations of invasive trades can be read not only in lists of businesses or maps of economic landscapes or the conversations of proprietors, but in the qualities of products themselves. Even simple T-shirts or computer-designed indigenous sweatshirts literally take shape as instruments of community life. Here again is a hidden connection among contemporary household producers in the northern Andes and the United States. To be sure, the link can be hard to see. Matched up against industrial products in the

US consumer economy, artisan goods came to matter for the individuality of each piece, the skilled handwork, the faithfulness to tradition, the expression of the artisan's own technique. But releasing artisan commodities from the need to always be contrasted with a factory alternative allows their features to be read for other stories. Designs begin to work at multiple levels, especially when commerce is rapidly changing. If the products are entirely new—say an invented indigenous art form—then artisans need to devise the constraints on their form and find ways to keep their goods intelligible. Alternatively, if producers are rapidly scaling up production, they must find qualities that can translate across technologies. Individual designers need to develop techniques of exclusivity and secrecy to protect the profits of their designs. Yet, as they enrich themselves, they must also be able to show where their designs circulated and strengthened the community trade for others as well. For artisans, the shared nature of their working life materializes in the designs, materials, and qualities of their goods, even those made on computerized power looms or with industrial sewing machines.

Who Are the Artisans?

Of course, given these lessons—of how intertwined artisans are with risk, uncertainty, capitalism, the nation-state, invasive trades—it is reasonable to ask what then differentiates artisans from industrial capitalism. When they work on computerized sewing machines and electric power looms, how do you know an artisan when you see one?

Indeed "being an artisan" is not a forever-fixed identity. Artisans are people who participate in particular kinds of work. As people change, and work changes, that work may very well no longer be usefully thought of as artisan. Nevertheless, most of the people we worked with in the northern Andes can be seen as artisans.

There are several facets of artisan work:

1. Artisans are members of *households*, incorporated into home-based enterprises and intertwining labor with kinship or kin-like ties.
2. Artisans participate in *cottage industries*, with a degree of autonomy or control over their work, tools, and materials, but subject to competitive pressures.
3. Artisan *work and skill* is usually more valuable than their tools, even though there can be significant mechanization and division of labor.
4. Artisans must in some way respond to the demand of *tradition or community*.
5. Artisans very often sell products of *indeterminate value*.

Households are crucial to artisan work, because in prosaic terms, artisan trades build from the household's "base" (Gudeman 2005). Such a base is immediately physical—the tools, workspace, and savings that lie close at hand and can be put to use. In the lore of North American innovation, the base is the famed entrepreneur's garage. In the northern Andes, it may be a table set up on the patio, the ground floor of a home, or space in the house of an emigrant neighbor. Perhaps more important, the base is social. The relations of the house—in particular those of a married couple—establish the guiding trajectory of the business. Indeed, the very form of the commodity can reflect a spouse's knack for design while the markets achieved highlight the selling skills of the other partner.

The household features in two other ways. First, artisan work will not neatly measure itself in the terms of a capitalist accounting of profit and returns on investment. In her study of family firms in Italy's silk industry, Sylvia Yanagisako (2002) insists on using desire and sentiment to analyze economic action in terms of the way the words point to identity and affect as business drivers. For the artisan, it is sentiment that causes difficult business and personal choices to blend—spouses, children, fellow artisans, and the wider community get mixed up in market days, machinery purchases, or new product lines. As Heather Paxson (2013) points out, this is not just a private matter. Artisanship generates an economy of sentiment that figures across suppliers, producers, wholesalers, and customers and makes it impossible for an artisan to operate "under the weight of a single overarching ideology" (Paxson 2013, 92).

Second, born of the household's resources, the artisan enterprise creates concern about succession from the start. Children grow up becoming skilled at tasks in the business. To the extent the enterprise succeeds, parents must grapple with how assets will be passed on to their heirs. Faced with an ailing industry, an artisan must appraise current decisions in terms of debts and forsaken opportunities passed on to children.[3]

This type of household business is a *cottage industry* because it is never exempt from pressures to increase work and compete for sales. Detailed ethnographic work from the 1970s and 1980s explained how artisans ramped up "petty commodity production" (Chevalier 1983) as rural regions fit ever more tightly into the global capitalist system. In making cloth (Smith 1984a, 1984b), bricks (Cook 1986, 1998), pottery (Nash 1993), hammocks (Littlefield 1978, 1979), and decorative textiles (Annis 1987; Stephen 1991), artisans labored, accumulated savings, and reallocated their time away from farming and toward products that would yield a profit. Inspired by Karl Marx and Soviet agrarian economist Alexander Chayanov, researchers analyzed the perils of self-exploitation in unpaid domestic labor, the flight of economic value as artisans sold commodities at dirt-cheap prices subsidized by their own subsistence production, and the emergence of exploitative wage relations within communities.

Artisan *work and skill* are always at the heart of the enterprise. The skills are tacit, learned in the doing, by hand and handed down (Ingold 2000, 2013). Nevertheless, producers have long mechanized what they could. Weavers of sashes gave up backstrap looms for the efficiency of treadle looms (Meisch and Colloredo-Mansfeld 2007). Poncho makers disassembled treadle looms to make space for electric powered jacquard looms (Meisch 2002). Even where all production is human powered, artisans break down tasks that can be reorganized within the house to increase output (Chibnik 2003) and connect to other households to increase sales (Milgram 2000). At some point with all the machines, the hired labor, the repetitive designs, and mass marketing, the artisans stop looking like an alternative to industrial production. Yet the social stature and cultural world of becoming an "industrialist" never materializes. Physically located in the building where a family lives, the shops are officially registered as artisan, and those who labor there rarely receive formal worker protections.

Indeed, for all the machinery and specialization, artisans never free themselves from *tradition or community*. Partly, tradition is there to be mined, the way Malian artists used the tradition of Bogolan mudcloth to inspire fashionable African shirts or inexpensive tourist items (Rovine 2008). Other artisans are like jazz musicians; versed in customary styles, they improvise new ones. In the Colca valley of Peru, for example, men and women who embroider skirt borders learn dozens of varieties of a standard repertoire of motifs and from there will combine them with a style glimpsed in new printed fabric, or images from a book, or a detail seen on an old colonial building (Femenías 2004, 131–32). With artisanal food in the United States, old European recipes can give contemporary American cheese makers a jumping-off point for new farmstead cheeses with an instant pedigree (Paxson 2013).

The force of tradition frequently comes from outside. Consumer expectations of tradition and authenticity shoehorn many rural manufacturers into kitschy market niches. The goods are meant to conform to an imagined timeless standard. Even when the craft or product in question is less than a generation old, such as the woodcarving trade of Oaxaca, Mexico, producers go along with the stereotype of tradition because "the sellers know that crafts sell well when they fit into a romantic narrative that places the maximum cultural distance between artisans and customers" (Chibnik 2003, 243). In economies involving native peoples or open-air markets or sales from farms or country stores, clients will accept a bewildering range of novel items as traditional simply based on the setting of the sale.

Invented or not, tradition is not always about a trade's past. The creation of a tradition of production to hand down may become its own aspiration. In his account of the spread of woodcarving in Oaxaca, Chibnik warns against taking too sentimental a view of artisan work. He observes that for carvers, "although artisans take pride in their work, they almost always say that they make pieces in order to make money and would abandon the craft if the market for carvings disappeared" (2003, 6). This caution is important, but so is the condition "if the market for carvings disappeared." Once a community does invent a trade, then claims of tradition may be used to keep the market from collapsing. In Peru, potters have won from the government formal trademark protections to ensure that ceramics devised in the mid twentieth century would have an edge against future copycats and knockoffs (Chan 2011). The claims are made for local residents, not just tourists—they elevate artisan investments as a moral decision, one that not only returns profits to the owner but preserves the craft and endows the next generation with the work.

Artisan products are also often curious artifacts, with *indeterminate value* at the point of sale. Some involve a great deal of work and investment and yet become worthless at the market. Other products with similar work and investment can command high prices. This difference is often through sheer luck or timing, although that luck can sometimes be converted into enduring market share. In a winner-take-all economy, one producer can become the go-to artisan, while a host of others—enabled by the relatively low start-up costs and nourished by hopes of the big payout—crowd at the edges, creating the look and feel of a traditional artisan economy.

So these are the artisans of this book—men and women working with others in their households to produce commodities. They seek to turn a profit and invest to expand earnings. Yet as economically driven as such actions are, the artisans are also part of an obliging connection to their community. Their manufacturing may place them in a line descending from parents and grandparents; it also may be handed down to their children. In the chapters that follow, we look at how this happens with an eclectic sample of contemporary Andean material culture: indigenous paintings, pigs and potatoes, woven sashes, cabbages, T-shirts, embroidered shirts, acrylic sweaters, and Pow Wow–themed sweatshirts. In their own ways, these goods and the work they involve carry the history of the community and characterize the families who churn them out.

We document the social playing out of artisans as invasive trades. Chapter 2 clears the ground of some common stereotypes regarding peasant agriculture and artisan production. Evidence from long-term fieldwork and historical accounts overturns the stereotypes of conservative, risk-averse peasants or of traditional, low-output artisans. Rather, risk and market sales have for centuries been inherent in peasant and artisan endeavors. The emerging artisan economies in the last few decades certainly drew upon, and continue to be intertwined with, the agricultural market plazas so typical of the northern Andes.

This risk-taking is inseparable from the competition that drives the markets. And in the 1990s heyday of market-promoting policies in the Andes, rewards of competition in modest provincial trades ended up looking like the wildly skewed payoffs of Hollywood's winner-take-all star system. In chapter 3, we document this dynamic. We find that many accounts of competition have treated its effects too narrowly. It is in fact this lopsided competition that can be a crucial element for the spread and routinization of new artisan economies.

For these artisan economies, accusations of imitation and selling copies too cheaply reflect the bitterest moments of competition. Chapter 4 examines the fate of designs in Otavalo, one of Latin America's largest artisan economies, looking at the life of innovation in an open-air market with no formal intellectual property protection. We discover that unregulated ideas are not "free," in the sense that they do not conform to the logic of rapid diffusion, exploitation, and obsolescence in an open market. Moreover, amid the stealing of designs, the lost earnings, and the mutual suspicions, artisans were also materializing the shared value of their goods.

Chapter 5 traces a related but different route to a public economy. In the 2000s, Atuntaqui's quality improvement program was designed to leverage the power of strategic cooperation and bring the hidden factories of hundreds of family businesses up to global levels of productivity. Government officials and international consultants socially engineered competitive advantage and social capital. Over the course of the initiative, however, social interactions became more inclusive and more contentious. An invasive trade became a routinized and public basis for an invaded community, although the dangers of reprivatization reveal lessons and risks for this public economy.

In chapter 6, we return to the story of the Otavalo wedding shirt to demonstrate how bold innovation draws from cultural wellsprings and how entrepreneurial energy can return to a community. This chapter uncovers the intrigue of the intellectual property and design claims of three women—an apparel producer, fashion designer, and an embroiderer—who created President Rafael Correa's shirt. Their creativity, understandings of copyright, and economic plans for the shirt illustrate important currents of Latin America's postneoliberal economies.

Adam Smith and the Artisans

In praising the artisans of Brooklyn, Adam Davidson made a thoughtful connection to Adam Smith. The artisan payoffs, he implies, are found in the world of small producers, specialized and expert in their trade, who are promoting the public good through independent dedication. However, there is more than that to learn from the Scottish philosopher. Adam Smith's observations, although often used to justify all kinds of industrial capitalist activities, had more to do with eighteenth-century artisan enterprises in rural Scotland. There is a great deal to be recaptured from Smith's descriptions, which predate by a century the melding of unidirectional market-and-evolution models.

Adam Smith's pin makers, for example, would be quite at home in the pages of this book. The workshop at the heart of Smith's famous discussion of the division of labor was a small, very poor manufactory. They had second-rate machines, and the ten men who worked there had to take up to two or three different jobs in the making of the pins. Yet, so organized, they churned out their wares: 48,000 pins in a day. And around those plying the pin trade, others worked in manufacturers, both trifling and great, so that all of industry can be understood as a division of labor, and all of society derives its advantage from the truck and barter of so many occupations.

In his reflections, Adam Smith always intended his 1776 economic treatise, *An Inquiry Into the Nature and Causes of the Wealth of Nations*, to be read together with his 1759 essay on morality, fully titled as *The Theory of Moral Sentiments; or, An essay towards an analysis of the principles by which men naturally judge concerning the conduct and character, first of their neighbors, and afterwards of themselves*. Together, the works portray a society in which individuals do pursue their self-interest, yet they are beholden to each other, morally, emotionally, and materially. Indeed, Smith is reluctant to reduce empathy for others to a kind of pure self-regard. He writes that even if one rejoices when one sees that another man shares one's passion or grieves that he does not, the connection between the two men is unbidden and automatic: "the pleasure and the pain are always felt so instantaneously" (1982, 14). And when it comes to work and markets, even if each manufacturer pursues his own gain, in his commercial life, "man has almost constant occasion for the help of his brethren" (1981, 1:18).

What emerges in these works is a nation of individuals at once separate and yet dependent on each other for their well-being. Amid this condition, Adam Smith famously derives the public good from the individual's effort to direct his or her industry for personal gain and thereby providing what society most prizes of the effort (1981, 1:477). Smith finds the multitudes of producers involved in gain-seeking exchange sufficient for promoting the common welfare. Years of working in markets built by peasants and artisans in the Andes have taught us this is not the case. If commerce creates mutuality, if it intertwines fates—and we agree that it does—it sets people on a course to debate what commerce alone is not providing. Offering the truism that a producer needs the help of the other men and women who ply their trade, Smith observed that, "it is vain for him to expect [help] from their benevolence only" (1981, 1:18). This is the heart of the matter. The power of lessons from the invasive trades and historically invaded communities of the northern Andes is to teach from whence this help comes, and why.

Fast Easy Cash: Artisan Risk and Peasant Markets

To understand artisans—whether in the northern Andes or as a trendy prescription to fix contemporary capitalism—we need to clear out common preconceptions about what artisans do. People often imagine artisans as carrying out low-risk, routine activities outside of markets and capitalism. Together with small-scale farmers, or peasant agriculture, this rural and small-town life epitomizes notions of traditional society. We intend to demonstrate in this chapter the amount of risk that is actually involved. Artisan and peasant activities do not stand apart or outside of capitalism, but have been tightly intertwined with markets for a very long time. The artisans' responses have not been just to hedge against the worst case, but to make a play for the best.

To make this case, we first discuss how the people of southwestern Colombia, a rural region of small farms and artisan workshops, became engulfed in a financial pyramid scheme promising big returns that were fast, easy, and in cash. Closer investigation reveals how small-scale rural farmers—peasants—who often have been depicted as excessively conservative and traditional, have been enmeshed in risky ventures and dramatic market fluctuation. Subsequent chapters discuss how the rise of artisan producers and vendors in Ecuador was similarly based on risky gambles and exchange-rate arbitrage. This chapter shows how these artisans would already have been quite familiar with risk taking from experience with peasant agriculture in the northern Andes.

We then examine why analysts and accounts of traditional societies have so often overlooked risk and markets. This takes us into some crucial misconceptions that arose during the European phase of industrial capitalism, and an anthropology that drew on these misconceptions. We return to the northern Andes to posit that artisans and peasants are quite flexible when it comes to risk and have long had a symbiotic relationship with market sales. Peasants and artisans generally undertake risk in moderation, a finding that parallels the discussion of innovation in chapter 4. While we can certainly admire artisan values, we should keep in mind the vulnerabilities that make risk a part of artisan endeavors.

From Peasants to Pyramid Finance

The Andean highlands of southwestern Colombia had long been a peaceful refuge from Colombia's notoriously violent urban slums and areas of guerrilla conflict. This region at the northern edge of classic Andean patterns is dominated by small-farm or peasant agriculture: potatoes, cabbages, corn, and wheat, together with larger farms dedicated to dairy cattle. Túquerres, a small town and regional market center, exemplified the continuities of small-plot, manual-labor peasant agriculture. That would change in the early 2000s when several wealthy landowners enlisted paramilitary units and the US-backed drug war of Plan Colombia revealed drug-smuggling operations extending from the Amazonian region through the highlands and to the coast. The situation then calmed, and in 2009 it was possible for us to revisit the region and follow up on earlier anthropological fieldwork undertaken in the 1990s.

The continuities of peasant agriculture can be very reassuring.

Revisiting Túquerres revealed familiar sights—people were still growing potatoes, selling produce in marketplaces, and working in artisan shops. However, and somewhat surprisingly, people insisted this apparent normalcy had been reestablished only recently—that just one year before, everything had been different: "no one planted"; "no one worked"; "we sold our pigs"; "we lost everything." Southwestern Colombia had been engulfed in the frenzy of putting money into schemes that became known as *las pirámides* (the pyramids).[1]

In retrospect these were clearly gigantic Ponzi schemes, with classic pyramidal structures destined for collapse. In Túquerres, the largest scheme, which was perhaps the largest in Colombia, was known as ***Dinero Rápido Fácil y Efectivo*** (DRFE; fast easy money in cash). It was difficult to believe that these sober agriculturists—people who put money into pigs in lieu of banks—had been drawn into such schemes. How could they have sold their pigs in order to speculate in such ventures?

Stereotypes and images of peasant agriculture or small-farm life are almost always about continuity, of risk-averse subsistence in a traditional society. The very word "peasant" suggests a conservative, traditional, nonmarket subsistence producer. Peasants are almost by definition averse to innovation and risk taking. Subsistence-oriented peasants endure in anthropological accounts, from Eric Wolf's classic *Peasants* (1966) to James Scott's *The Moral Economy of the Peasant* (1976). In a detailed look at the way sharecroppers in Brazil planned their regular crops and their small farming experiments, Allen Johnson noted, "the workers of Boa Ventura consistently pursue the low risk strategy for one simple reason: if they fail at the high risk strategy, they may starve. Not merely capital but their very livelihood is at stake" (1971, 135). Scott employs a stark image of a peasant as "a man standing permanently up to the neck in water, so that even a ripple might drown him," insisting that "subsistence-oriented peasants typically prefer to avoid economic disaster rather than take risks to maximize their average income" (1976, vii).

We do not dispute these authors' preoccupation. Risk haunts

peasant livelihoods. But reflecting on what happened during southwestern Colombia's pyramid scandal reveals how willing small farmers may be to assume risk and uncertainty, in part because they had already participated in such farming and agricultural sales in the northern Andes. Even in the 1990s, there was more change and market-oriented activity than met the eye, but only in retrospect does a closer reading of farming ventures confirm that they had never actually been the risk-averse peasants the literature sets them up to be. One reason people in the northern Andes could get caught up in these risky pyramid schemes is that they were already familiar with taking risks in peasant agriculture.

Let's start with pigs (see figure 6). In Túquerres, a family would buy one or two little pigs approximately every four months. The pigs would live in a concrete pen behind the house, fed on food scraps. If all went well, a pig could fatten and double in value in four months. Sales were typically coordinated to events like the start of school or Christmas festivities, so some of the proceeds could be spent on school supplies or fiesta preparation and the remainder could be reinvested in a new pig. Then the cycle began again.

This small-scale pig trade seems to be an ideal example of how peasants prefer building assets in real, tangible items. (Rather than bank accounts, these were literally piggy banks, investments on the hoof, true pork bellies.) In the course of fieldwork in the 1990s, Jason purchased a "research" pig. This purchase led to interesting discoveries. Pigs are not owned by the family as a whole, but individually. One individual in the family may be the owner of the pig, or as in the case of the research pig, people may go in halves, splitting the cost of purchase and at the end splitting the proceeds. There may be other family members involved in feeding the pig and getting the pig scraps, but they would not have a claim on proceeds.

Also, not all pigs grow fat. People might buy two pigs together of roughly the same size, keep them in the same pen, and feed them the same food, but one may grow nicely while the other

FIGURE 6. A country pig (Photo: Rudi Colloredo-Mansfeld)

does not. This leads to conversations and reflections on pigs—all the guessing and estimation that goes into trying to discern which pig will grow nicely, and of the times that a certain pig had gotten fat or one pig never fattened. Even two brother pigs, born in the same litter, can have dramatically different growth rates. And of course, pigs can be stunted by disease or die.

Perhaps most importantly, pig prices swing dramatically. With many households making similar plans, selling pigs for holidays or school supplies, those could be the very months when pig prices hit bottom. People try to time the market to sell at the high points, but that was uncertain: plans are plans, school supplies must be purchased, and fat pigs become a liability when they begin eating everything in sight, outpacing the household scraps and demanding purchased sacks of potatoes just to be kept alive.[2]

The research pig did not do well, suffering from slow growth and poor market timing. The initial price was 70,000 Colombian pesos, higher than expected, and five months later it sold for 110,000 pesos, lower than expected. After expenses of almost 10,000 pesos on medicines, purchased pig scraps, and carrots, the piggy bank did slightly better than an interest-bearing bank account, but not by much. With all the time spent buying, feeding, selling, and caring for the pig, as well as the risk of disease or death, the interest-earning bank account looked pretty attractive. Fattening livestock turns out to be far from a sure-thing investment. As local residents said, we had been testing our *suerte*, our luck, for raising pigs. The test failed, and no one offered to go halves with an anthropologist on a research pig again.

As with pigs, so too potatoes. In the mid-1990s, there was an incredible run-up in potato prices, to levels no one had seen before. People would shake their heads in wonder at the prices people paid for potatoes. They talked about saving the potatoes out of the lunch soup for a dinner meal. One woman said she used to buy a sack of potatoes, eating the big ones and throwing the little ones to the pigs, but "now the little ones are for us—[we are] the pigs." Even *El Tiempo*, a national newspaper, complained: "It is at least paradoxical that the price of a tuber ruined the most sophisticated expert projections" ("La Meta de Inflación se Cumplió para los Pobres," July 3, 1998).

Of course, high potato prices could be good for farmers and agricultural workers. Lots of people began planting potatoes, hoping to reap large gains. One man who usually planted cabbage turned his small plot to potatoes. During the potato frenzy, he emphasized he was planting potatoes "so they'll be in the house," but he was also doing the mental calculations of how much they would save over market prices.[3] He would in one sentence describe how much better the potatoes would be than market varieties, talking about how they could not be found in the market, and then in the next sentence describe how much he would have to spend on chemical fertilizers and pesticides to grow the potatoes.

Eventually potato prices moderated—potatoes planted at the demand peak were harvested at much less than had been hoped. "Everything is like that here," a market vendor explained, pointing at people carting boxes of tomatoes into the market plaza. "Those were expensive, but now they're cheap." The man who had turned his backyard plot to potatoes had seen them ruined by a night frost. He said this was why he preferred not to plant crops on the scale he once did. It was simply too risky. He preferred agricultural day labor, even at low wages, no benefits, and enduring times when there was no work at all. Still, this felt more guaranteed than the wrenching boom-and-bust of small-scale agriculture.

A similar dynamic afflicted some of the farmers with larger holdings. In general, they did not have the same worries as small-holders, as their larger plots of land could be planted at varied times. They could also benefit from integrating potatoes and dairy operations—potatoes helped make the ground suitable for better pasture. Some dairy farmers said they did not care about potato prices, claiming the income was just a side benefit to soil improvement for pasture. Nevertheless, one of the largest potato farmers in town had apparently begun from rather humble beginnings and made lots of money through several key harvests. A few years later, people said he lost everything through unlucky crop failures and market timing, and that he was only slowly building back his potato operations. Older potato farmers talked about price fluctuations going back to the 1960s, and how one harvest could be a make-or-break proposition: "Two sacks of potatoes went for around 30 or 40 pesos. Forty pesos when they moved the most. Then there were frosts around Bogotá and the price went to 220 pesos. I had potatoes. I made a million pesos."[4]

And again with cabbage. Cabbage was a favorite crop for people planting tiny backyard plots. Even miniscule plots offered the potential of two selling opportunities for the cabbage: as seedlings to be transplanted to fields with larger holdings, or at maturity. During a windfall, proceeds can go to fashionable tennis shoes, jeans, a birthday-party dress, or high-heeled pumps. But at other times, "there is no market" for cabbage and families eat what they can, letting the rest rot behind the house.

One cabbage transaction illustrates these swings, described by a producer who also purchased cabbage so his mother could sell it in regional market plazas. This producer and marketer told how he began by offering 100,000 pesos for a plot of cabbage, but the two producers with a sharecropping arrangement wanted 350,000. He then went to 120, 140, 150, and stopped at 160,000. The producers said they would not accept less than 200,000 and ceased negotiations, but the next day they relented. He said that when prices were high, the lot could have gone for 700,000. Others reported that the producer had thrown sacks of cabbage over a cliff when they could not be sold.

And it is not just Colombians who see such swings in fortune. In a paper titled "Corporation: A Peasant Strategy for their Relationship with the Changing Global Order" (2010), Patricia Torres shares examples of risk seeking and risk management from smallhold farmers in the Philippines, Mexico, and elsewhere. For instance, Torres cites a conversation between researcher Orlando Chacón López and a peasant farmer in Toluca, Mexico:

> We take risks . . . three years ago I invested six million pesos in carrot farming and I lost them because the harvest did not prosper due to bad weather, but the following year I invested ten million pesos in the farming of the same product and I earned fifteen million pesos. It's like this here, you have to take risks because today you lose but tomorrow you win.

Torres details how peasants use corporations to defend peasant livelihoods. She considers this corporate strategy as potentially very old, as perhaps predating Spanish colonialism, but certainly part of "the emergence of the world capitalist system during the Spanish Empire."[5]

In striking contrast to stereotypes about risk-averse peasants, small-scale agriculture can be an endeavor saturated with risk and uncertainty. Even the smallest plots are integrated with market prices, and market prices fluctuate substantially. The pyramid finance scheme did not introduce risk to naive peasants: they were already quite immersed in it from agriculture. And, in relation to the speculative borrowing that took place in highland

Guatemala in the 2000s, the fast, easy, and in-cash speculation of Colombian potato farmers seemed almost rational.

With detailed portraits of lives from the Cuchumatanes Mountains of western Guatemala, David Stoll (2013) offers harrowing accounts of loansharking, real estate speculation, and costly migration to the United States. In the 2000s, international agencies began to promote the ideals of low-interest microloans as a pathway out of poverty. Guatemala's Rural Development Bank and local credit unions operationalized the ideal by making tens of thousands of loans, not just for micro amounts of less than $1,000, but for amounts up to $6,400. And even as the loan amounts swelled, rural Guatemalans looked for ways to leverage the loans and ramp up the returns. In one case, a woman named Ingracia launched a scheme in which she induced fifty other women to take out loans and turn the money over to her. In return, she offered them an upfront cash gift and a promise to repay the loan. Stoll estimates she amassed $125,000 before absconding with the money.

At a loss to find profitable investments for their loans, households would turn around and re-loan their microcredits to others who promised to sponsor migrants to the United States and pay the loan off with remittances. In one case, a couple borrowed approximately Q500,000 from their neighbors (at 7.8 quetzals to the dollar, that's US$64,000). Turning it over to four men known to advise young migrants, the pair expected to reap millions. Stoll reports that "what they didn't know is that their partners invested the funds in, not emigrants or projects, but a Mam Maya priest who promised riches from the volcanoes of Quezaltenango" (Stoll 2010). In the 2000s, Cuchumatanes became an economically toxic blend of land scarcity, population growth, credit, borrowing, and emigration. The details of the cases—gifts of money among neighbors, priestly investors—were novel, but the linking of peasant households to high-risk ventures was happening in other regions of Latin America. And while pyramid schemes had become new engines of wealth destruction in Guatemala and Colombia, the basic behavior of peasants caught up in such schemes has a long precedent. Many participants in the pyramid schemes in Túquerres said they were going for one more month, and then they would have sold their shares to enjoy the holidays or pay school tuition. Just as they had done with pigs.

The Tradition-Bound Peasant in Tradition-Bound Political Economy

Subsequent chapters discuss how the rise of artisan economies in Ecuador similarly involve risk and innovation. Here, by connecting dramatic stories of pyramid finance to the basic calculus of peasant agriculture, we hope to show that risk was not a new thing for these artisans. Smallholder agriculture in the northern Andes has long been intermeshed with calculations of economic windfalls and breakdowns. In his thoughtful review of peasant economic choices, Michael Chibnik (2011) points out that small-scale farmers are adept at dealing with not only the known unknowns (risk) but the unknown unknowns (uncertainty); peasants and artisans continually diversify and experiment in the face of such perils to expand the fortunes of their enterprises. Tiguan painters began selling to airport tourist kiosks (chapter 3), Otavalo merchants traveled the world to sell sweaters (chapter 4) and Atuntaqui textile producers turned their town into a fashion mall (chapter 5). None of these producers were recent entrants into markets and capitalism. They all knew quite a lot about risk, market transactions, and capitalism from their roots in peasant production and peasant marketplaces.

Indeed, given the long history of peasants within the global capitalist system, it is worth retracing how markets, money, and risk were obscured. In the nineteenth century, as industrial capitalism resulted in wrenching changes for European countries, peasants were seen as a last stronghold—for better or worse—of a noncapitalist, nonmarket, traditional conservatism. Two highly influential analysts, giants in the establishment of the social sciences, solidified these ideas. The first is Karl Marx's 1852 depiction of French peasants in *The Eighteenth Brumaire of Louis Bonaparte*:

The small-holding peasants form a vast mass, the members of which live in similar conditions but without entering into manifold relations with one another. Their mode of production isolates them from one another instead of bringing them into mutual intercourse. . . . Their field of production, the small holding, admits of no division of labour in its cultivation, no application of science and, therefore, no diversity of development, no variety of talent, no wealth of social relationships. Each individual peasant family is almost self-sufficient; it itself directly produces the major part of its consumption and thus acquires its means of life more through exchange with nature than in intercourse with society. A small holding, a peasant and his family; alongside them another small holding, another peasant and another family. A few score of these make up a village. . . . In this way, the great mass of the French nation is formed by simple addition of homologous magnitudes, much as potatoes in a sack form a sack of potatoes. (1963, 123–24)

Most people would not readily quote that description or trace it to Karl Marx. Still, it is remarkable how this description precisely fits what many people persist in believing peasant life to be— even if those French peasants, like the people in the northern Andes, had been buying and selling in marketplaces for centuries (Braudel 1982). The durability of this mistaken idea leads some to proclaim that peasants have disappeared because crops are sold in a marketplace.[6] It would seem that every time peasants enter a marketplace they cease to be true peasants—even if the marketplaces are run by the very same peasants!

A second source of this mythology is Emile Durkheim's book on *The Division of Labour in Society* ([1893] 1984). Durkheim claimed that there were two types of social relationships arising from the division of labor: organic solidarity and mechanical solidarity. Then, in a turnabout that would confuse students for years to come, Durkheim said that preindustrial society should be seen as mechanical solidarity, because everyone was doing the same kind of work, like identical parts of a machine. Industrial society, for Durkheim, had organic solidarity, because people did different kinds of work and had to relate to each other like parts of an organism.

People do not today often quote Marx on the French peasantry or Durkheim on forms of solidarity. However, these descriptions from Marx and Durkheim distilled a basic groundwork for divorcing industrial economies from peasants and artisans. The early luminaries of anthropological research reinforced such a division.[7] One of the first and most famous ethnographic accounts, Bronislaw Malinowski's *Argonauts of the Western Pacific*, set out to slay the idea of "Economic Man." Malinowski lavishly described the fascinating trade circle of the Kula ring, with shells and armbands circulating around the islands, but he paid little attention to the *gimwali*, or bargaining barter. Malinowski said Trobrianders viewed barter with scorn (1984, 96). Many anthropological accounts were typically conducted as far afield as possible and anthropologists sought to rescue and recapture the logic of activities conducted outside markets.

The idea that peasants aimed first at a risk-averse strategy to satisfy subsistence needs went a long way to explain what others derided as irrational backwardness. The containment of risk became a foil to recover the rationality of peasant investments. The more researchers could show the containment of risk, the more sensible the artisan and smallholder appeared. Studies detailed effective, often ingenious, hedging strategies related to diversification, reliance on local breeds and crops, and moderate experimentation to incorporate potential new winners.

This approach has a great deal of merit—after all, these are societies that were said to not have viable systems or logics of any sort. The apparently irrational behavior was a colonizing justification to seize land, exploit resources, and conscript labor into the global economy. In this context, anthropology correctly defended alternative approaches to economic organization and priorities other than market-based capitalism. If anthropologists did not do it, who would? Or, as Michel-Rolph Trouillot calls to anthropologists:

We owe it to ourselves and to our interlocutors to say loudly that we
have seen alternative visions of humankind—indeed more than any
academic discipline—and that we know that this one ... that con-
structs economic growth as the ultimate human value ... may not
be the most respectful of the planet we share, nor indeed the most
accurate nor the most practical. We also owe it to ourselves to say
that it is not the most beautiful nor the most optimistic. (2003, 139)

Consequently, after a century of anthropology, market logics seem
to always be only recently arriving and inevitably corrupting in
places like the provincial Andes. Peasants are predominantly portrayed as economic naïfs—timid, vulnerable, and prone to flight
at the sight of capitalism's financial machinery. This is probably
why when economic game-playing experiments became a research fad, a first question tackled was "Are peasants risk-averse
decision makers?" (Henrich and McElreath 2002). The answer,
culled from the results of the economic games, was that peasants did not seem to be risk-averse.[8] Experimenters could have
come to the same conclusion by a more thorough review of the
anthropological literature on peasants.

An early example of this literature is Sol Tax's *Penny Capitalism: A Guatemalan Indian Economy* (1953), which explored peasant life using principles from economics. In fact, Bronislaw Malinowski's final field study—described as *Malinowski in Mexico:
The Economics of a Mexican Market System* (Malinowski and de la
Fuente 1982)—concentrated on this market immersion. In Peru,
Jacques Chevalier's *Civilization and the Stolen Gift* showed how
home-grown crops may "have an exchange value without ever
being exchanged" (1982, 118). David Lehmann documented an
agricultural boom in northern Ecuador since the 1960s, mainly
driven by small and medium landholders, which had commercialized the family relationship: "the picture offered here is of a
family farm in which certain devices exist to match the returns
to individual members against their contributions. . . . When
sons leave school they do not work for free on their fathers' land;
rather, they sharecrop with him" (1986b, 621).[9]

Yet, even as research has shown how much of peasant life is market life, writers rarely do justice to the verve of these producers—the amount of risk they are willing to stomach, and just how much they want to earn. Indeed, even when insisting that peasants are market oriented and profit seeking, Samuel Popkin's argument in *The Rational Peasant* is for a rather staid operator—peasants become quasi-accountants who calculate the balance of short- and long-term investments to "raise their subsistence levels" (1979, 4).

But peasants and artisans have dreams too. Pennies may be the initial investment of some, but the payoff they seek can well be in dollars, sometimes thousands of them. And their capitalism is not just basic market behavior of buying low, selling high, and investing in new land and equipment. They seek loans, take on debt, leverage exchange rate differences, and lock in advantages of scale. In Ecuador, the artisans of Otavalo have long been the models for this behavior.

Sprouting from the success of their Plaza de Ponchos, Otavaleños are premier examples for embracing risk and new investment to continue economic expansion. Even considering the concentration of resources and people in market vending and textiles, the expansion of trade and techniques is impressive. They have set up shop in Europe, the United States, and in other Latin American and Caribbean countries (Meisch 2002). Back home, they have brought new products and techniques to the Plaza de Ponchos, including subcontracting sweaters from distant non-indigenous towns, adopting embroidery work from other indigenous communities, and investing in power looms and machine production. If Thomas Friedman were searching for an example of how an entire economy may benefit when everyone becomes an artisan, Otavalo would be an ideal slideshow.

However, the Otavalo success can be difficult to explain, since fortunes in this artisan economy seemed to swing independently of the national economy. Otavalo's trade had been growing countercyclically, expanding substantially from the early 1980s until the late 1990s when Ecuador itself struggled through periods of inflation, falling wages, and financial crisis. One long-time sweater entrepreneur, Gladys Arias, is an especially telling example of someone who earned a big payoff during Ecuador's "lost decade" of financial stagnation. Gladys and her sister had begun to make versions of hand-knitted, Irish-style sweaters in natural colors. A young man from Britain who had been importing some crafts from the Otavalo market contracted with the sisters to deliver more sweaters, advancing them the funds to buy wool.

With new operating capital, the sisters contracted with other knitters. Few could be found close to home, so the Arias sisters drove three hours north to the province of Carchi, near the Colombian border, and went in search of potential clients who had stayed put in potato-growing households. Here was penny capitalism and the risks involved: a piecework knitter received from $1.00 to $1.25 per sweater and Carchi agriculture offered other profitable alternatives. At first the sisters had to beg the knitters to work with the thick wool. Until then, the producers had used soft, brightly colored acrylic fibers for sweaters. None of the Carchi women had seen people wearing the bulky, coarse garments they were being asked to knit.

In talking about these early days, Gladys still seemed weary from the women's resistance to working with rough, dull wool and larger sizes. "We had so few colors to work with, brown, greenish brown, and *caca de vaca* [cow manure]." Desperate for more variety—not least of which to keep up the morale of their producers—the Arias sisters bought dyes and experimented in their kitchen, soaking wool in solutions of pigments, salt, and lemon. Gladys shook her head looking back on her ignorance.

In the early 1980s, the sisters were able to recruit about thirty producers and it would take days to bump along the rough roads to reach them all. Gladys said that they wanted to work with more women, "but it was difficult in those days because people had what they needed to feed themselves to buy whatever little thing they wanted." In fact, the same commercial potato cultivation that expanded fortunes in Túquerres was booming on the

Ecuadorian side of the border. Carchi women had no reason to take on more knitting work when their households were profiting from potato yields.

Gladys continued: "But the economic situation in the whole country started to fluctuate and people began to lack things. Prices went up. Rural people began to feel a need for cash. Thus, this was the cause that they [the women of Carchi] began to work a little. It was a good moment for us. The exchange rate of the dollar was better, going up ahead of the sucre's fall. The economic crisis of the country increased even more and so the women began to work."

By the end of the decade, the sisters had 800 knitters working for them. Other British designers sought them out. They had an exclusive deal with a chain of more than fifty stores in the United Kingdom and had to work with shipping brokers to arrange shipping containers from Ecuador's premier port city of Guayaquil for their orders. They earned in hard currency, saved, and then paid their expenses with the ever-devaluating national currency. Gladys recounted all this while sitting in the bright sun on the edge of a burbling fountain in the courtyard of a large, traditional house that she and her sister had bought in the middle of the town of Otavalo. With richly painted adobe walls, tile floors, and quiet porches, her house could have been a museum. The long bleak years of driving through the drizzle of Carchi with a pick-up truck laden with skeins of cow-shit colored yarn had paid off handsomely.

Sitting in his darkened workshop, Luis Ramos offered the flipside of the sweater trade: the risks he had taken turned out for the worse. He too had started as an intermediary of woolen goods but then switched out of hand-knitted woolen goods as the market became saturated in the mid-1990s. Ramos aimed at a piece of a new market: machine-knitted, acrylic fiber sweatshirts with llamas, Inca suns, mountains, and stylized condor motifs. He first bought a $10,000 rebuilt Korean machine and eventually earned enough to secure a deal on a $20,000 unit. Trying to keep up with the investment of the other twenty or so families in the trade, Ramos then bought a towering $75,000 rotary machine in 1998.

The next year, Ecuador's largest banks began to fail, the national government devalued and then abandoned its currency, and the Otavalo craft merchants lost their hard currency advantages. Ramos tried to innovate his way out of his cash crunch, coming up with a bold new design for his sweaters. Rivals immediately copied it and it went on to be one of the most widely used designs in 2001 (a story picked up again in chapter 4). With his sales collapsing, he tried to sell his machinery, but by 2001 no one wanted to expand production of acrylic sweaters. The $125,000 he had invested in his workshop was lost. But Ramos seemed unfazed by this disaster. When talking about the end of his run as a sweater producer, he figured he would eventually sell the machines. He thought perhaps he would invest the proceeds from the sales in a greenhouse and try his hand at commercial vegetable growing.

Piecework: Replacing the Risk-Averse Stereotype with Risk in Moderation

With these stories of pyramid schemes, potato ventures, cabbage cultivation, and sweater dealing, we hope to release peasants and artisans from stereotypes of risk-averse drudges. But we do not want to overdo it. As with most matters in rural communities, risk provokes a range of response across a social group.[10] Thus "risk in moderation" rather than "risk seeking" or "risk averse" might be a better starting point for tracking trends in the provincial Andes.

Now back to the pigs. The black-and-white pigs fattened in Túquerres were known as "creole" pigs. Some residents considered getting pink pigs, known as "monkey pigs" because Colombians use the term "monkey" for someone with light skin and hair. The agricultural school selling these pigs called them an "improved race," ready for market in half the time of creole pigs.

But most eventually decided the initial price was too high, particularly since the new pigs might get sick. They stuck with a known potential earner rather than an uncertain new one. And even in 2008, when residents started to sell off their livestock and move into the pyramid scheme, most did not "lose everything." People told stories of other people who had "lost everything": selling cars, houses, and land in order to invest in the pyramids. But none of the people interviewed had actually lost everything. They bet their pigs, not the farm. They did "lose everything" in the sense that everything invested in the scheme evaporated, but few went as far as mortgaging a house or land.

There have been researchers who stress this more middle-of-the-road approach, showing how peasants take risks, but selectively. This is the approach Nola Reinhardt emphasizes in Colombia:

> In general, the farmers of El Palmar were selectively integrating elements of the technological innovations into their existing agricultural systems. In addition to the new crops and varieties and their associated inputs, farmers were experimenting with the use of fertilizer on traditional crops (maize/beans, coffee). With selective adoption, they achieved some income gains with minimal risk; in doing so, they forfeited the greater gains that might have been achieved with a riskier strategy of full-scale technological innovation. (1988, 205)

In other words, peasants experiment at the margins, taking chances that money will line up for a specialty crop, knowing that the sale price may crash if others are chasing the same dream. However, if there were similar price fluctuations in the "traditional crops" of maize, beans, and coffee as to those that occurred in potatoes, cabbage, and carrots, it is not entirely clear that this is a minimal risk strategy, nor that they were necessarily forfeiting greater gains.[11]

There is both something old and something new in attending to risk, speculation, big payoffs and financial meltdowns in peasant and artisan economies. On the one hand, there is an odd replaying of Max Weber's discussion of Protestants and Catholics in the opening of *The Protestant Work Ethic and the Spirit of Capitalism* (1958). Weber notes that the proverb jokes, "either eat well or sleep well," drawing parallels between a Protestant's willingness to risk much for his gains and a Catholic's acceptance of relative poverty for untroubled earnings. The peasant, then, is cast in the role of the Catholic: venturing little, eating gruel, but rarely going hungry.

However, by the end of his essay, Weber effectively shows capitalists to be both eating well and sleeping well in their routine careers. Sustained by their rationality, they pay their price in the absence of joy, not presence of worry. For peasants and artisans, though, "market" and "rational," have often been uncoupled. Calculation and routine, whether in sizing up new business options or in tried-and-true artisanal production, does not guarantee returns in the long run. Put another way, even with a set of creative hedging strategies, their risks are much more than minimal. Consequently, rather than always having an eye on the downside, many willingly assume large amounts of risks in the hope of the upside.

But the 2000s also turned out to be a newly intense decade of risk taking, speculation, and pyramid schemes. On Wall Street investors invested in group funds that in turn invested in operations that were nothing more than Ponzi schemes. Internationally, microfinance mechanisms were touted as the powerful new tool to alleviate poverty. Neoliberal orthodoxy of the governing parties in Colombia and Ecuador prescribed entrepreneurship and competitiveness as the path to progress. Again and again, people seemed to pile on to some new venture.

This kind of risk taking carries a particular material signature. When household after household in a rural sector bets on cabbages, the hillsides become pocked with patches of their pale green leaves. When sweater merchants place big wagers on acrylic fiber production, knitted sweatshirts swing on hangers from shop after shop down the commercial thoroughfares of Otavalo. Returning to a farming community or a provincial streetscape caught up in one of these speculative moments, it is akin to an invasive species taking over. Risk has come to manifest itself in a new product saturating the landscape. Ultimately, the mutations, variations, and successful new generations of these products reveal how risks are tamed, who reaps the big payoffs, and how the historically invaded communities accommodate a new sorting of winners and losers.

Winner-Take-All Competition: How Artisan Stardom Sustains Artisan Production

Tourists to Ecuador see a lot of Tigua paintings, from the airport kiosks to people hawking paintings in the streets and parks of Quito, Ecuador's capital city. There are upscale versions priced in the thousands in boutique folk-art galleries and cheap $4 souvenirs in the Otavalo market plaza. The Tigua paintings are composed on a sheepskin canvas with bright, enamel house paints—they seem to epitomize folk art (see figure 7). Colorful scenes of fiestas and rural lives dramatize Corpus Cristi celebrations and the arid, open landscapes of the Andean highlands. You've made it to Ecuador—it's hard to resist picking up a commemorative painting, maybe at the last airport kiosk.

The Tigua paintings are curious. Although the artistic themes appear to draw heavily on Andean traditions, folk art, and rural life, the paintings are a relatively recent innovation—they have always depended on the tourist industry and international connections. By now, that should be a familiar story—curious, but not a surprise. Elsewhere in Latin America, ethnographers have charted the recent inventions that have launched and sustained

FIGURE 7. Toros del Paramo, 2010 (Painter: Nelson Pilatasig, used by persmission; photo: Rudi Colloredo-Mansfeld)

such crafts: Oaxacan woodcarvings (Chibnik 2003; Brulotte 2012), Zapotec weaving (Wood 2008), Otavalan sweaters (Meisch 2002), and Chulucanas ceramics (Chan 2011). For all their newness, such crafts quickly gather meaning for their producers. As they chase the tourist dollars, these carvers, weavers, knitters, and potters debate among themselves how their wares carry community tradition and who among them really deserves respect for their creativity. Following the discussions, anthropologists show how quickly new artisan products can become vessels of identity and ties of a community.

Another curious feature of Tigua painting is perhaps more surprising: even though a whole valley of peasants-turned-painters fills every market niche, and the painters themselves have formed multiple artist associations to develop their trade, the earnings from Tigua paintings have concentrated in the hands of just a few painters. In the 2000s, there were two particularly successful households: one in the upper Tigua valley that was home to a renowned painter who championed the vision of his father, Julio Toaquiza, the founding artist. The other household was in Quito and a major hub of distribution for a wide network of rural and urban painters. Meticulous sales tracking, often quite difficult to come by for artisan endeavors, reveals an income concentration comparable to Hollywood stars, fiction authors, and investment bankers. Few researchers have grappled with the mechanisms of such skewed payoffs. How is it that a trade so tied to community in terms of its inputs, skills, and identity becomes so individualized and lopsided in its rewards?

This chapter explores the implications of this winner-take-all competition for artisan crafts. Perhaps paradoxically, the winner-take-all payout is at least partly responsible for spreading and sustaining the artisan sector: it is the basis for how artisan work crosses a threshold to become an invasive trade. People see the possibilities of a big win—dramatically illustrated, dramatically visible. They can see the means to that end, and so there is a piling-on effect, with more and more people joining the craft. Although there may be only a few big winners, there is just enough hope to keep plugging along, especially in the absence of alternative visions or alternative visible routes to success.

We begin with accounts of brick makers, belt weavers, and sweater manufacturers to provide background on the uneven earnings that we have found. Whereas risk taking is a centuries-old component of artisans' connection to capitalism, this winner-take-all aspect seems newer, emerging mostly within the last few decades. Winner-take-all competition signals not just new tactics among artisans. It is also a sea change in their livelihood, as local goods aim for national markets and earnings from all over the country or niche markets from around the world funnel back to a socially bound collection of specialized producers. It is becoming a pattern for artisan economies, the rule rather than the exception, as is true for many professions around the world.[1]

Neither anthropology nor economics has adequately explained why these tournament earnings should be showing up among what otherwise looks like old-fashioned, putting-out-style cottage industry. We try to understand how previous explanations have fallen short and also provide new ways to interpret the durability of a winner-take-all system. As we link the winner-take-all competition to relatively recent globalization, we also seek to adjust some common misconceptions about how competition works.

Competition in artisan economies is not exactly what development planners and market advocates thought it would be, nor is it exactly what some academics and anticapitalists rail against. Indeed, artisans often invert common ideas about competing. To begin with, competing successfully is predicated less and less on objective economic factors of capital and innovation and more on expressiveness, communication, and cultural affiliation. Second, the competitive dynamic is frequently not one of go-it-alone individualism, but positioning; of reading neighbors' successes and aligning with them, even while seeking to come out ahead. Consequently, competition is better understood as a vital relationship among competitors than discrete acts of allocating winners and losers. Over time, this jockeying for position, disputing others' moves, and copying of success comes to constitute not just a market niche but a "field of cultural production" (Bourdieu 1993). It is a social space where stature can be gained, cultural traditions forged, and prosperity pursued.

Third, this essential *cultural* work of competition is not to sweep away the inefficient or to drive out lagging producers, but rather to reconcile the painful inequalities emergent within communities and their professed shared values. To see this, it helps to think about when such reconciliation fails. When people reject the legitimacy of someone else's big earnings they hint at cash-grabbing behavior that is not true competition. Beleaguered rivals speak of their successful peers' hidden sales of contraband or the treachery of their "disloyal competition," by which they mean dumping products for below cost. To leave a rival's gains undisputed as the results of competition is a sign of accepting others' good fortune even if it exceeds one's own. And to secure such acceptance, competitive strategy entails not just a play for earnings but also cultural action to embed those gains within a moral community. In the uncertainties of the rapid growth of an invasive trade, such care in competing is a crucial element of building a community from the raw hustle of the market.

Bricks and Belts, Sweaters and Paintings

At first, an artisan district appears incredibly uniform. Lots of small workshops, small retail shops, endless shelves, bundles, and racks of similar products. The surface uniformity suggests few opportunities for getting rich. Inequality seems muted. Yet for home-based industries, fortunes vary, if for no other reason than the life cycle of a household, which will see children grow—changing from consumers to workers—before departing to again diminish the household labor supply. And on the basis of even a temporary gain in family resources, greater wealth can be built. Take the example of the most utilitarian of all crafts, brick making. The anthropologist Scott Cook conducted an extraordinarily detailed investigation of brick making in Oaxaca, Mexico, in the late 1970s. He found that even among a group of brick-making families who had all similarly become owners of their own brick-yards, earnings varied considerably. The wealth of these family operations spread evenly from those still working hard just to recoup their investments to others who had substantial income stream from a profitable set of clients. The commerce in bricks yielded an even gradient of artisan prosperity (see figure 8).

Such findings, though, turned out to be a poor guide to the earnings of a different utilitarian craft in Otavalo twenty years later. On the fringes of the booming indigenous tourist craft economy of Otavalo, the belt-weaving community of Ariasucu seemed the textile equivalent of brick makers. Here, household-based operations manufactured a simple, useful product for sale to a nontourist, indigenous customer base. At the time they entered the trade, many weavers had little experience with producing textiles as a commercial commodity. Most men of the sector

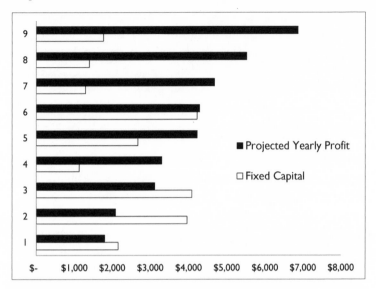

FIGURE 8. Brick maker incomes, nine independent brickyard operators, Santa Lucia del Camino, 1979 (Source: Cook 1986)

had instead started their working lives by traveling to Quito to work as laborers and masons during the oil-boom economy of the 1970s. When it came to earning their living, bricks were in fact far more familiar to them than belts. Then a deep national recession in the early 1980s made work scarce for Ariasucu's urban migrants. Like the Tiguan painters, they developed home-based handicraft production to fill their earnings gap. Ariasucu, one of the humbler outlier zones around Otavalo, became the center of this trade. A forty-five-minute bus ride from Otavalo, Ariasucu was a scatter of homes, some with cement-block construction, others with rammed-earth walls and among them a dozen or so empty, larger two-story houses built by absent migrants. Most locals were poor; inequality was muted. Left out of Otavalo's fast-growing tourist textile economy, the residents of this zone tried their hand at this undeveloped business.

Of all the items worn by indigenous women, belts had been the least commercialized. Belt making largely took place on old-fashioned backstrap looms between farming tasks. In the wake of land reform in the 1960s and the oil-boom economy of the 1970s, so many young men left their spouses and their looms to find work in the cities that women throughout the highland provinces had to go to market to buy fajas that were once woven in the home. Consequently, across the Andean provinces, an untapped market of tens of thousands of customers for fajas emerged.[2] The challenge lay in meeting new demand. Converting from laborious backstrap looms to treadle looms in 1978–79, two brothers in Ariasucu pioneered production techniques, simplifying the designs so that a weaver could take a standard loom used for ponchos, blankets, or shawls and set it up with four narrow frames hung on pulleys or with slices of rubber inner tubes to make a basic striped faja (see figure 9). The innovation boosted their belt production tenfold. The two brothers then traveled to Quito and provincial capitals selling belts to resellers who brought the belts to remote provincial towns. The brothers introduced a packet of innovations, but they were never financially successful. However, the weavers who trained in their workshop did prosper.

Indeed, throughout the development of belt making, innovation never conferred a lasting advantage on a single operation. While techniques rapidly evolved, the inventions mattered less for the big earnings they could deliver than for the respect and clout they brought their inventors. For instance, a former construction worker named Jaime Cuyo rose to prominence in the late 1980s, in part by devising the most intricate pattern yet developed: a diamond design that required a nine-pedal loom. However, in a community where competitors were also family, such designs never remained exclusive. Cuyo taught two of his brothers-in-law his design not long after he started selling it himself. Thus, even the fanciest fajas became more or less standardized commodities. Rather than defending the margins of a new product, Jaime Cuyo succeeded because he managed to find workers to keep eight looms in production churning out his diamond design.

After Jaime's gains, an operation run by Enrique Teran and

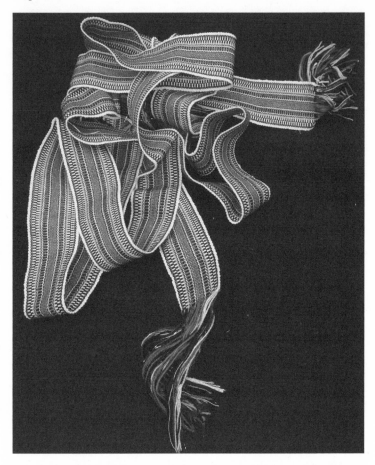

FIGURE 9. A faja in the simple design of the early treadle loom belts (Photo: Rudi Colloredo-Mansfeld)

Rosa Chiza emerged to dominate the market, even though they introduced no new design or labor form or material or marketing angle. Instead they excelled at recruiting and retaining workers. Only by sitting at their kitchen table in an old-fashioned, windowless, two-story rammed-earth, tiled-roof home and going through the inventory of their consumer goods did their wealth stand out. The stereo, televisions, refrigerator, stove, clothes, fur-

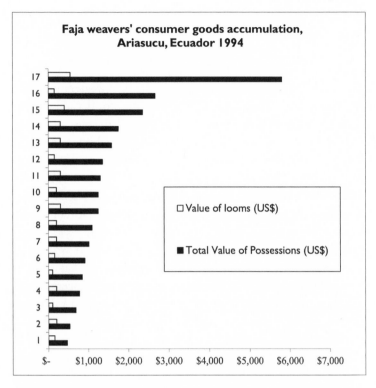

FIGURE 10. Distribution of faja weaving household wealth as measured by inventories of consumer goods, 1994

niture, and other items cost $5,801 in 1994 (see figure 10).[3] The next largest inventory was worth only half as much, while the median value of all dedicated faja weavers' households was $1,243 (Colloredo-Mansfeld 1999, chapter 5). Dozens of other residents had also rigged looms for fajas, but their rewards were even more meager.

Eventually, by the end of the 1990s, Enrique and Rosa revealed to the community what everyone had guessed. By local standards, they were rich. They built a three-story cinderblock house with broad tinted windows. On the ground floor, they stocked a store with soft drinks, crackers, cookies, and canned goods. In the next room they opened a business with four telephone cabins. Out front they parked three cars—two double cabin pick-up trucks and a hatchback, the vehicles that continue to help Enrique ply his trade in markets throughout highland Ecuador.

Down in Otavalo, another trade showed the same skewed payoff. Unlike belts, machine-knitted acrylic sweaters were the epitome of tourist-driven craft in the 1990s. For decades, ambitious Otavaleños had refined and expanded the production of hand-knitted wool sweaters. They partnered with foreign buyers to improve quality and traveled across multiple provinces to recruit knitters. The shift to acrylic came about in the 1990s. It was an Andean moment of disruptive innovation: the rise of a simpler, cheaper, inferior, more convenient product that remade the market (Christensen 1997). The saggy, sweatshirt-style acrylic sweater gave customers the basics of a native craft with their standardized Andean condors and llamas in an item that could fit into most European and American wardrobes. Producers mechanized, scaled up, and learned to run their machines day and night to meet big orders. Unlike most other crafts in Otavalo, acrylic sweater making had high capital costs—a basic setup of an industrial knitter, sewing machines, and other equipment cost around $10,000 in the 1990s. The larger shops had costs between $300,000 and $500,000 for knitting machinery alone. Few families could afford to enter and compete in the business. By 2001, the twenty-one families who had succeeded in this work operated on a scale unmatched by any other set of producers. At a minimum, they could churn out 750,000 sweaters a year if they could secure the orders.

A snapshot of acrylic sweater sales data in 2001 revealed the tell-tale skewing toward a single successful firm (see figure 11). To assess the hardships brought on by the fiscal reforms of 2000, known as the "dollarization" of the Ecuadorian economy, our research team had partnered with Otavalo's largest artisan union, the Union of Indigenous Artisans of the Centenario Market, Otavalo (La Unión de Artesanos Indígenas del Mercado Centenario - Otavalo; UNAIMCO). In a survey of producers, the research team recorded the quantity, dates, and destination of

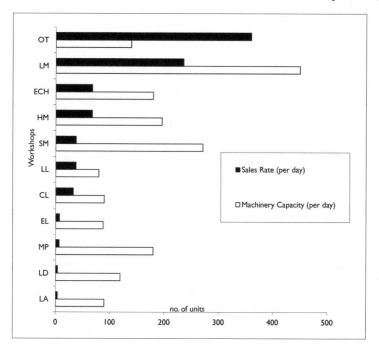

FIGURE 11. Sales rate of machine-knitted Sweaters, Otavalo, 2001

the three most recent sales by manufacturers and compared the sales rate to the shop's production capacity. One firm emerged in a clear expansionary mode, with demand exceeding their capacity for the surveyed time period. In relation to its next-closest rival, the top firm had one-and-a-half times the sales and only one-third of the machinery. When interviewed, the owner credited their success to a savvy family member living at the time in Spain and reporting trends in colors and designs back to Ecuador. Interestingly, she made no effort to hide these successful new fashions. Rather than exclusivity, she admitted that she copied designs from others, even as she displayed her latest on a clothesline strung above her showroom's front door. As different as her sweater operation was from the belt weavers up the mountain, she shared with those artisans a habit of openness.

Finally, the case of the Tigua painters. There are approximately two thousand Quichua-speaking Tiguans, dispersed among ten peasant sectors in their home valley of Tigua, as well as migrant communities in several Ecuadorian cities. Since the 1970s, Tiguans distinguished themselves from other peasants by embracing and commercially developing an art form invented by Tigua resident Julio Toaquiza. Working with folk-art gallery owners in Quito, Toaquiza drew on older art forms related to drums, fiesta costumes, and religious objects in the Tigua valley. His innovation was to put the renderings of dancers and landscapes on a stretched, rectangular sheepskin canvas that could be hung on a wall. Recognizable as folk art, they sold. The painting craft then spread through the Tigua valley. By the 1990s, hundreds of households had turned to professional painting, as full-time painters, part-time suppliers, or people who could paint more if demand increased. Virtually any man or woman could get into the trade with the purchase of a few enamel paints from a hardware store in Latacunga (see figure 12).

The Tigua painting profession split in its early years. The founding Toaquiza family committed to living and working in their rural highland community, but ambitious painters from

FIGURE 12. Nelson Pilatasig in his studio (Photo: Rudi Colloredo-Mansfeld)

other sectors in the Tigua valley moved to Quito. The first wave of urban painters formed an artist association in Quito and fought successfully for the right to sell art in El Ejido Park on the edge of the central tourist district. For neophytes and experienced painters, the park became their center of commerce, a place to exchange ideas, and a setting for establishing the reputation of a new generation of painters. Throughout the 1980s, Ecuador's recession pushed more Tiguans into the profession and the city. Yet, despite their new urban lives, the migrant painters would return to Tigua, often dressed in new finery—women in richly embroidered shawls, men in pressed slacks and leather jackets. There they would attend the fiestas and bullfights or oversee upgrades to their homes, such as tin roofs and gas stoves. There were so many households of painters that ten different peasant communities had set up artist associations.

For all the new entrants and inclusivity, Tiguan artists were winding up in an unmistakable hierarchy, with a few clear winners among many anonymous toilers. Interviews with the leaders of four artist associations, data from life histories of twenty-six artists and a survey of 559 paintings in Quito's main folklore galleries in 1999 revealed four layers of painters. At the base were the hundreds of Tiguans who had sufficient talent and interest to maintain membership in the artist associations. Most, however, painted only part time. At the next level, approximately ninety households earned their living from their art. Of those ninety households, about fifty earned approximately the Ecuadorian minimum wage.[4] Then at the next tier, approximately thirty-seven households earned consistently higher incomes of about twice the minimum wage, a rate allowing for some material advancement. These painters divide into two overlapping subgroups: one of "first-rank" artists and the other of intermediaries or vendors who sold others' works as well as their own.[5]

Two artists stand out. Alfredo Toaquiza, the son of the original painter, helps organize international exhibitions of Tigua work. Much of his reward has come in the form of international travel and sponsored trips to discuss Tigua art. By the mid-2000s, he had materialized his fame into a stand-alone gallery located on the main interprovincial highway connecting Cotopaxi to the coast—the only store dedicated exclusively to Tigua art. Starting some thirty kilometers away, signs announce its location, and tour buses know to stop in to see dramatic canvases of scenes from Alfredo's life, such as when he was wrongly jailed in Quito's notorious Garcia Morena prison. The visitors also pick from hundreds of premium-priced paintings.

The second leading artisan is Juan Luis Cuyo, a controversial figure who, together with his wife Puri Cuyo, has run the largest reselling operation from the mid-1990s until the present. They and two of their sons have operated six different sales posts in both Quito and the Otavalo craft market. Their three-story home in Quito has a wide tiled center hall where Juan Luis and Puri receive painters from all over Quito and those visiting from Tigua. Juan Luis welcomes people with a smile and a double-handed handshake so firm that he tips his visitors toward him, drawing them ever so slightly off-balance. Adjacent to their hall is a cluttered storeroom stockpiled with purchases from their visitors, as well as his own painting table. For despite all his success as an intermediary, Juan Luis paints ambitiously—his oversized paintings fetch the highest prices of all the art he sells.

The greater the familiarity one has with the community of painters, the greater one's feeling of wonder upon arriving at Alfredo's and Juan Luis's businesses. In the average Tigua studio, the artist may draw back a protective sheet to show a few dozen small canvases he has for sale. Arriving at Alfredo's, the visitor stands in the doorway while the artist clicks a switch, bringing banks of neon lights flickering to life over hundreds of paintings. In Quito, migrant painters work in cramped rooms, many in cement block shanties on the outer fringe of the city. Upon arriving at Juan Luis's house, young painters often whisper to each other, seemingly unwilling to disturb the quiet, clean stillness of the front hall. One operation is in the misty moorland of rural Cotopaxi province, the other in a sooty, working-class neighborhood of south Quito. Both sites are dense concentrations of art and money. The cultural and economic wealth of Tigua had settled definitively into the houses of these two rivals.

How to Not Explain Artisanal Winners: Tales of Drugs, Capital, and Media Stars

Julio Toaquiza sells a painted drum to a folk art dealer in the early 1970s; fifteen years later his son Alfredo's art is exhibited on three continents and he is traveling internationally to share his story. In the late 1970s in Ariasucu, two brothers work out the thread count and the frame rig on their treadle loom to weave a faja in an hour rather than a day. Twenty years later, one of their neighbors has what looks like a small car dealership funded with the profits from belt weaving. The big payoffs for the lucky few were being spun out of some pretty simple products by households with skill sets similar to those of their neighbors.

In fact, to return to mundane agricultural products discussed in chapter 2, winner-take-all competition was probably quite important in the rise of commercial potato production in the northern Andes. In the 1950s and 1960s in the region spanning the Ecuadorian-Colombian highlands, crops of beans, cabbage, and potatoes—now seen as traditional—were spurred by the innovative use of hybrid varieties as well as chemical fertilizers and pesticides. The big landowners were not the ones instigating change. Rather, it was small farmers or market intermediaries, often sharecroppers, some of whom were able to leverage the earnings to eventually become big landowners themselves.

Indeed, one sign that the potato profits were becoming really substantial for a fortunate few was the snide comments being made. Townsfolk voiced skepticism that a sharecropper could begin buying out other farmers with the profits of a few good harvests: "There must be drugs with those potatoes—you can't make that kind of money from potatoes."

Wealthy handicraft entrepreneurs faced the same accusations in Otavalo. The suspicions were often rooted in the racism of the provincial Andes. Mestizos would look out on the multistoried homes and new cars in indigenous communities and announce, "These Indians, these Indians are moving drugs." Having once dismissed indigenous people as poor and dirty, some townsfolk preferred to traffic in stereotypes rather than really explain the peasant-artisans' newfound wealth.

These kinds of accusations have a lot to do with uncertainty about how artisan and agricultural markets function. Accusations of drug running are in part a misunderstanding of the winner-take-all markets, but it was not only local observers who struggled to make sense of the quick rise of a few successful earners. Anthropologists found it difficult to place them within their theoretical frameworks.[6]

In the 1970s and 1980s, anthropologists continued marketplace studies and investigating what were termed "petty commodity producers," an abstract phrase meant to cover both peasant and artisan production. Much of this research was located in the Caribbean and Latin America, drawing on pioneering studies of peasant marketplaces and thinking through a Marxian framework. Anthropologists began noticing the emergence of winner-take-all patterns. In 1984, Carol Smith put it succinctly and bluntly: "Does a commodity economy enrich the few while ruining the masses?"

For many anthropologists, the answer was "yes." Consistent with a Marxian framework and a disciplinary commitment that tended to tell the tales of those who had been ruined, anthropologists explained the emerging inequalities by asserting the primacy of capital. Some anthropologists argued that a segment of the artisan community can accumulate wealth through strategic use of wages, subsistence agriculture, and the terms of trade between producers and merchants (Friedmann 1978; Littlefield 1978; Kahn 1980; Stephen 1991; Tice 1995). Scott Cook, for example, points to small-scale, "endo-familial" accumulation, which allows some weaving and brick-making enterprises to get ahead (Cook and Binford 1990), although the "hegemony of merchant capital" frequently limits artisans' chances for real advancement (Cook 1986, 79). From the 1980s, with the institution of what were called neoliberal or promarket reforms throughout Latin America, anthropologists regularly asserted that a commodity economy was ruining the masses. The imposition of "market logic" was to blame for the jarring inequalities.

The anthropological analysis and accompanying denunciation of Latin America's neoliberal era was not necessarily wrong, but it left out several important pieces of the story.[7] Much of the denouncing was done on the basis of imagining that people only recently had been introduced to a market economy. The denouncers tended to miss the centuries-long involvement of peasants and artisans with markets and capitalism. The denouncers did not pay enough attention to the full picture of anthropological literature on markets (see chapter 2), and too quickly assumed that market logic alone would inevitably ruin rural and native peoples. Put differently, for the question of how a commodity economy was "ruining the masses," the masses became the ethnic and indigenous people anthropologists studied, while "enriching the few" became associated with national and international elites. However, this formula missed the fact that those enriched few could be members of ethnic or indigenous groups. Moreover, if a commodity economy does "enrich the few," then there is still the question of what it is that enriches the few to begin with. What makes an artisan prosper?

Explaining artisan and peasant enrichment simply on the basis of capital accumulation too often comes up short. In her study of weavers in Totonicapan, Guatemala, for instance, Smith (1984a) details how the town's commodity-producing peasants rose to prominence as "the most market dependent peasants in Guatemala." By specializing in ethnic clothing used by Maya women throughout the country, they exploited a market that grew with the urbanization and dislocation of Maya populations from relatively self-sufficient rural communities. Yet as the trade grew and concentrated, it produced an unexpected sort of accumulation. Unable to capitalize their operations, the peasant weavers "have not differentiated into two classes (although they have greatly differentiated with respect to income)" (Smith 1984a,

61). In Smith's sample of the largest-scale weavers in Totonicapan, the most prosperous netted $7,350, while the next highest income was little more than $4,000 and the median income sat at $2,807 (see figure 13).

In short, a few artisans were getting rich, churning out products and capturing a lion's share of revenue from the trade. The wealthy entrepreneurs with all those orders of goods going out the door, the new pickups parked by their workshops, and the regular house remodelings revealed these market-spawned hyper-artisans. And this very newness seemed to signal that they

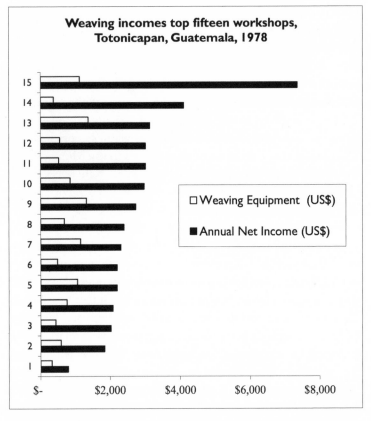

FIGURE 13. Comparison of earnings among weavers in Totonicapan, Guatemala (Source: Smith 1984)

were poised to detach from community or ethnic allegiance. Yet, across these cases in Guatemala and Ecuador, the big earners do not transition their wealth into capital. They do not lock in rents or profits from ventures they own. Class differentiation thus always seems incipient in such communities.

In other words, the break never comes. They remain in the community, making do with incremental additions to their machinery, seeking ways to make more out of the work they know, the social networks they shape, and the clients they attract. They stay home. More to the point, they stay artisans, and the lever of their wealth is to be found more in their households and community than in raw capital. At the heart of this yet-to-be-explained paradox are the workings of competition itself, not simply as a contest for earnings but as a structural tie among fellow producers who share trade, location, and identity. As these ties afford opportunities and the learning of trades, they also sustain a mechanism of terribly skewed earnings.

Becoming #1

Some economists have offered thoughtful accounts of just why winner-take-all dynamics or tournament-style earnings have been spreading from a few rarified occupations into mundane professions across the globalized economy (Frank and Cook 1995; cf. Colloredo-Mansfeld 2002). In the explanation of classical economics, significant gains in earnings would be attributed to significant innovation. In an imagined Adam Smith world of pure competitive markets, prosperity will go to pioneers—those who create new products, revolutionize techniques, and open up markets (Frank 1999, 146).

But in contrast to these easily available explanations, researchers have noted that in the highly competitive world of entertainment, some pop stars and movie celebrities earn far more than their peers without, in fact, offering much that is new or different. It is quite a stretch to claim that a particular voice or smile or special effect is double or triple the quality of peer competitors.

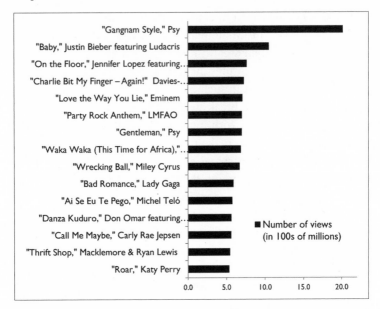

FIGURE 14. YouTube's most-watched videos, 2014

Talent, though, is a distraction when it comes to explaining earnings; position is what matters. In the contest between Korean artist Psy and his hit "Gangnam Style" (whose video on YouTube had 2.02 billion views as of June 15, 2014) and Canadian Artist Justin Bieber and his hit "Baby" (1.01 billion views), Psy's effort commands an audience simply for having commanded an audience: being number one has meant everything (see figure 14). Consumers who seek both to be entertained and to be trendy look not just at the quality of the art but the rank of the artist.

In fact, opting for the top of the list is efficient: it relieves buyers of having to know much about the rest of the people on it or the full range of what is on offer. In reality, "number one" may be only minimally better than a lower ranked alternative—say James Cameron's film instead of Steven Spielberg's (see figure 15). Yet the reputation as "the #1 film in America" ensures much greater earnings. With ever more consumers involved, through globalization or rising incomes, the lottery rewards typify a wide range

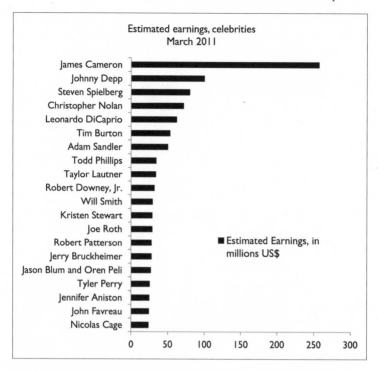

FIGURE 15. Estimated earnings among Hollywood celebrities (Source: *Vanity Fair* 2012)

of occupations. What began with pop stars and professional athletes then spread to investment bankers, lawyers, architects, chefs, and university professors (Rosen 1981; Lazear and Rosen 1981; Frank and Cook 1995; Frank 2011, 148–55).[8]

Digital technology intensifies this winner-take-all dynamic. In the rapid growth of Internet commerce, a single firm can make a fortune if it can become the standard platform for its category of service: Microsoft's operating system, eBay's auction site, Facebook's social network. Often referred to as network economics, the very fact of shared usage of a single product makes it that much more valuable to all users and creates a virtual monopoly for the lucky firm that owns the standard. Alternatively, the emergence of supply chains dominated by a few enormous corporations—Walmart or Sysco, for example—concentrates other payoffs. Shelf space is limited and the number of products that need access is growing. The producers favored by major distributors will gain disproportionately over their rivals.

But this is precisely what is odd. For all the reasons that Walmart, Hollywood, and the Silicon Valley deliver the big pay-off, potatoes, woven sashes or painted sheepskin should not. Artisan enterprise is supposed to be family-scaled, earning in proportion to the labor of the shop and face-to-face marketing. For an artisan, media reports usually offer little to help individual positioning. Journalists, travel writers, and scholars often focus on tradition and common motifs without describing any individual's body of work (Kirshenblatt-Gimblett 1998, chap. 1; Steiner 1994). Tigua painters have appeared in several publications and exhibition catalogs.[9] However, painters dismissed the economic effect of this attention. As one painter succinctly put it in 1999: "The people of Tigua, we have fame. But for each one of us, we have nothing." Even for the founding Toaquiza family, few buyers realize the stature Julio or Alfredo have within the painting profession.[10] For an anonymous artisan-vendor household such as Puri Cuyo and Juan Luis Cuyo, the dynamics of positioning are even harder to square with standard models of tournament earnings and networked economics. Clearly, though, they have found a hidden lever to a large share of painting profits.

In a way, the answer is straightforward. The wealthy artisans gain a set of subordinate painters who dependably produce for them. For example, a record of transactions during a six-week period in June–July 1999, revealed the core of Juan Luis's and Puri's supply network: four painters in two Quito households worked full time on smaller, souvenir-type paintings; a skilled member of the Toaquiza family who taught art courses and sold to galleries diverted some of his work to Juan Luis for quick cash; and somewhere between five and eight households from the newly subdivided neighborhoods south of Quito showed up once each during the period with small inventories of between ten and fifteen midsize canvases. Each month these painters would produce between 120 and 200 paintings, available to sell wholesale to Juan Luis and Puri. Over time, many of these clients approached them to become the godparents to their children.

These ritual relations of co-parenthood reveal just how many families have come within one household's network of producers. For example, in the Tigua-painting community of Quilotoa, one of the three men who first began to paint in the 1980s formed a business tie to an innkeeper north of Quito who was decorating his guest rooms with Tigua paintings. The Quilotoa painter began working with others and used his money to build a backpacker hostel near the rim of the Quilotoa crater lake. As his painting and tourism fortunes grew, more and more people asked him to be the godparent to their children. Years later, in 2013, the Quilotoan painter's daughter told me that she stepped in and begged her father to stop accepting any new compadre requests. She saw that baptismal celebrations and other compadre obligations had led to so much drinking that he was on the path to alcoholism and unable to work properly anymore. At the moment of her plea, her father had fifty-three godchildren, an enormous potential pool of support.

Once a large base network of suppliers elevates an artisan's inventory and cash flow, other benefits accrue. The central artisan can attract higher quality inventories than his rival. In 1999, a Tiguan migrant family had to raise money to hire a lawyer to get a relative released from jail. The surest way they knew to do it was to take their finest paintings to the resellers who had readiest cash: Juan Luis and Puri. The top artisan-resellers also draw the deep-pocket buyers. For Tiguans, these are foreign dealers who arrive at the El Ejido or Otavalo markets looking for a large Christmas inventory or folk-art gallery owners willing to pay a premium for a steady supply of the best quality paintings. To gain such clients is like securing a contract from Walmart—a demanding client who commands a lot of time and effort and delivers the kind of earnings that transform an operation.

In Otavalo, earnings growth was similarly self-perpetuating. Unlike the putting out system of Tigua painters, where subordinate painters equipped their own studios and delivered finished goods, the belt weavers mobilize labor more directly by hiring youths to come and work looms within the household's workshop. Teenage boys formed the backbone of the workforce in the 1990s. Earning the same piece rate in any home they might work for, the young weavers were lured not by the wage differences but by other enticements. They wanted to go to the busiest shops, places where a crowd of other boys might work. A boisterous workforce meant companionship and distractions. In the active workshops, the weaving itself was more pleasurable, as high-volume sales meant big inventories of spooled thread to vary the colors and designs running through their looms. The successful weaving households cranked out not just products but worker entertainment, with high-priced TVs and stereos blasting through the workday. Once again the trick for the artisan was to put in motion this self-reinforcing cycle: the more young weavers that join the house's workforce, the more others want in. The boys want to work for number one.

In reality, for artisans there is nothing very complicated about the mechanisms of big earnings. Indeed, it is the simplicity of them that makes it challenging to explain why one particular artisan comes out on top. There are always others within a trade who could easily assume the top place, and from time to time positions switch: Enrique and Rosa in place of Luis Jaime; Juan Luis Cuyo in place of the Quilotoan. The fact that such reversals of fortune happen within extended families of the peasant-artisan social world, where envy and grudges can become sources of lasting enmity makes positional competition that much more fraught—and that much more interesting.

The Unfinished Business of Competition and Reconciliation

Tiguan painters are acutely aware of the enormous earnings of a few resellers. At about the time Juan Luis Cuyo's brother-in-law used his profits to buy the first pickup truck in the community of Quiloa, a backlash set in. Resenting the market dominance of

Juan Luis and his ilk, some artists refused to sell to them. Members of two large artist associations pushed for a formal prohibition on the reselling of another artist's work. The critics felt that resellers not only exploited poorer painters, but corrupted the way competition and their self-made market in native art itself was meant to work. The argument resulted in a divisive atmosphere that crippled the work of artist associations for years afterward. The challenge to a specific economic practice (a painter's reselling of another's art) threatened the whole field of cultural production (Tigua painting as authentic indigenous art).

To understand this crisis of legitimacy, it is helpful to return to key elements of Bourdieu's analysis of art, authenticity, and economy. Rejecting a narrow sociological explanation of art and class interests, Bourdieu (1993) attended to the wider sets of social relations that exist among artists. He insists on two elements necessary to the maturing of art into a field of cultural production. First is the autonomy of the field. It has its own symbolic rewards, means of elevating standing that are independent of earnings. Second is the contest among practitioners themselves—the continual "position taking." This sets the boundaries and rewards of the field. Position takings are decisive acts in relation to art, style, and politics. At times, position taking is orthodox and affirms the core accomplishment of the field. At other times the artist's move is heretical, boldly recovering a rejected practice or borrowing alarmingly from an unrelated art.

In his work on Zapotec weaving in Oaxaca, W. Warner Wood (2008) draws from Bourdieu to show how a community of artisans builds up over time through multiple plays for position and acceptance. "Every practice makes claims about legitimacy," Wood observes (2008, 18). What is made and how it is made, where something is sold and who sells it, when earnings get spent and on what—each of these is a moment in which an artisan authenticates his or her work. Unlike Bourdieu's artists, for whom the very autonomy of artistic production lies in the rejection of economic logic, artisan bids for stature and acceptance entail embracing skilled economic action. Artisans contend with a far more intimate connection between economic ambition and cultural production. Thus in their "position taking," artisans wind sequences of market transactions into an ever tighter relationship with expressive practice. Cultural accomplishments in the realm of painting, fiestas, cuisine, and personal fashion become a foundation of commerce, while the promotion of market activities can renew artistic effort.

In the fight over the legitimacy of reselling, rival painters took positions about everything from legitimate competition, artistic contributions, and economic solidarity among residents of the parish. In 1999, several years after the tensions about reselling flared up within the artist associations, the issue of fair business practices was still hotly discussed by painters and resellers living in Quito. Interviews and conversations revealed the fault lines and fallout.

For many of the original Tiguan painters who had pioneered the move to Quito and selling in El Ejido Park, competition is acceptable as long as it occurs among artists and not businesspeople. When explaining the time of creative development in Tigua art in the 1980s, one leader of an artist association said, "there was a lot of competition among us. We came to the park [to sell our paintings] and tried to make a good presentation. There was a lot of improvement." This painter blamed the rise of intermediaries for a subsequent decline in creativity: "Since 1990, members of our own communities have worked like intermediaries. There have been a lot of changes. Because of the intermediaries, because of the competition, technically speaking, our painters cannot improve." This painter wanted a return to inclusive marketplaces in which artists sought to win customers through their own creativity.

The wealthy intermediaries rejected the claim that they limited the market for others. Instead, they pointed out the real economic benefit they delivered: their reselling provided steady income for rural Tiguans. A young painter and reseller pointed out, "A painter goes to the folk art galleries in vain. I had a painting of the first quality, 15 by 20 centimeters. I took it to the gallery 'La Bodega.' They offered me only 20,000 sucres. An intermediary would pay 45,000 sucres." As the debate developed, the parties seemed to reverse Bourdieu. The older "anti-reseller" painters wanted to restore Tiguans to face-to-face market competition for the sake of their art; meanwhile, the intermediaries promoted intracommunity exchange for the sake of indigenous ideals. Another intermediary pointed out that resellers' purchases allow an indigenous married couple to live together. He said, "I once went with my cousins to sell clothes in Colombia. We worked for days and sold nothing, not one thing. For weeks we walked, we suffered. This painting work is tranquil. With it, one can live with one's wife, peacefully with one's family. If we do not do this, what do we have?" He went on to point out how hard it was to be a reseller. "We do not have capital like someone selling in the galleries, who can buy and store and buy and store paintings. We have to get out and sell them or else we cannot buy."

The resellers' deepest claims to legitimacy rested on their own status as painters. Time and again, vendors stood up at public meetings to insist that they sold their own work first, not just other works, and that they not only painted, but painted well. The reseller who pointed out how hard it had been in Colombia and how hard he worked to resell paintings also rejected the idea that he was "only a businessman." "I have been to Canada. My art has been at a university in Vancouver," he reminded everyone, speaking of the inclusion of his paintings in a museum exhibition at the University of British Columbia in 1998. For his part, Juan Luis Cuyo stopped painting anything but the largest sizes in 1999. Among the hundreds of paintings in his storeroom, he had only four of his own but each was at least 100 by 80 centimeters in size and all priced at around 400,000 sucres (approximately US$125 in 1999), nearly ten times what he charged for his average paintings. He would point out the quality of his work and the ambition of his subject matter. "These are the complete fiestas, everything that there is."

Beyond the debates about fair competition and beyond the art, resellers made small and large bids for acceptance based on their roles as economic and social patrons. Early on a weekday morning in July 1999, Juan Luis Cuyo finished a transaction to acquire eight paintings from a young couple and then turned to pierce their infant daughter's ears. His hands shook with his nervousness. Unwanted, this ritual responsibility had fallen to him by dint of being the girl's godfather. More grandly, a rival intermediary contracted with a band from Cotopaxi province to come to Quito to play at the wedding of his godchild, a fiesta that would draw together the wider community of migrant Tiguans. As the musicians led the wedding party down a muddy lane from a raw, new cement block church back to the groom's house, the Tigua parish came to life in Quito in the parade of about forty-five men and women, many with narrow brimmed fedoras accented with peacock feathers.

The provincial wedding band, the tiny earrings for an infant goddaughter, the wide and detailed canvas. Artisan earning power remains inseparable from such position takings and the relations they cultivate within their communities. More than that, the communities grow from this cultivation. Social activity, work, and ritual arise precisely where the most enterprising entrepreneurs objectify their ambitions. The successful artisan creates the social fields where stature can be achieved. As newcomers follow suit, they operate in the styles and locales devised by the successful entrepreneurs. Complying with the standards set for the marketplace by established leaders, for fiestas and for personal consumption, newcomers seek to take their own positions and their own way up the hierarchy. In the chain of moves and positions, competition has become a "forcefield of human interaction" in which contending notions of accumulation and obligation are being adjusted and through which expressive forms are improvised (Jackson 1998, 14). That is, in competing, people materialize their belonging and struggle to legitimize the disparities that such belonging entails for themselves and for others.

Small Operators, Big Winnings, and Artisan Communities

Economists have moved beyond explaining the drivers of such skewed earnings to laying out the social costs. Robert Frank has been an especially acute critic. He sees in all these positioning struggles a kind of Darwin economy (2011) in which everyone sinks more and more of their income into positional goods, seeking to gain an edge in school admissions, entry-level job interviews, and so on. Others also see growing incentives to intensify work, including for those at the top as an "increased inequality and tournament style economic system that gives the person who puts in an extra hour of work a potentially high return" (Freeman 2008, 137). Thus for some, the winner-take-all economy is one more path to drudgery. Still others find the roots of alienation: "In the ever more elongated upper tail of the income distribution, it is the logic of tournaments that determines the distribution of prizes, and tournament winners feel little obligation to sympathize with the losers. As the star system spreads to other occupations, as in academe, the same tendencies show up there as well" (Leijonhufvud 2008, 121–22).

In a recent best-selling reflection on the implications of winner-take-all economies, *The Black Swan: The Impact of the Highly Improbable* (2007), Nassim Nicholas Taleb makes a rough division of the world between *mediocristan*—places, communities, and economies where "winners get a small segment of the total pie"—and an *extremistan* of "winner-take-almost-all effects" (2007, 36). While Taleb considers mediocristan to be more typical of past or traditional societies, he recognizes that an increasing number of domains resemble extremistan. Indeed, although this description comes from the Internet economy, it could very well characterize what we describe as invasive artisan trades:

> The small guys, collectively, should control a large segment of culture and commerce, thanks to the niches and subspecialties that can now survive thanks to the Internet. But, strangely, it can also imply a large measure of inequality: a large base of small guys and a very

small number of supergiants, together representing a share of the world's culture—with some of the small guys, on occasion, rising to knock out the winners. (Taleb 2007, 224)

Taking a broad view, Taleb sees in the winner-take-all dynamic the opening of the economic margins that perpetuate small-time artisan trades—the long tail of low earners carving up the market of consumers indifferent to the allure of "number one." Such artisans can make it as long as they can maintain their skills and sniff out an untapped niche. Some may nurture hopes of making the big time. Once in a while, someone does.

In his 2012 follow-up, *Antifragile: Things That Gain from Disorder*, Taleb considers artisan activities and artisan products more directly as potentially antifragile. For one thing, artisans

> have some volatility in their income but they are rather robust to a minor professional Black Swan, one that would bring their income to a complete halt. Their risks are visible. . . . Thanks to variability, these artisanal careers harbor a bit of antifragility: small variations make them adapt and change continuously by learning from the environment and being, sort of, continuously under pressure to be fit. (2012, 84)

Moreover, artisan products tend to be less fragile than those that are technologically produced: "What is artisanal has the love of the maker infused in it, and tends to satisfy—we don't have this nagging impression of incompleteness we encounter with electronics" (2012, 324).

On its surface, Taleb's praise of the artisan economy and the artisan product seems parallel to Thomas Friedman's injunction that we all need to "think like artisans." It is another idealized view of personalized production. However, in contrast to Friedman, Taleb's artisan is face-to-face with risk. Taleb is not lecturing us on the hard-work virtues of artisans as a solution to economic woes, but rather looking for alternatives to winner-take-all extremistan—a relief from the payoff structures that Friedman himself enjoys.[11]

Taleb, though, underestimates the degree to which many artisan economies now participate in winner-take-all extremistan. At the same time, he overplays the producer's own hand in creating a measure of their robustness. For with artisans, the adaptation is not simply the activity of an individual shop. Antifragility is also an outcome of inter-artisan ties.

The stories of paintings and belts point to lessons about how an artisan trade takes off in an invasive surge but then routinizes as a new community tradition. First, there is a quantum leap in the available earnings: a national market rapidly grows for an indigenous woman's belt; international folk art collectors become interested in a new art form. Second comes the dramatic win, the surprising success that nevertheless draws on skills that are latent in the community. This dramatic win is important. It is the prize held out for risking so much time on a craft that has taken on a strange new form amid unfamiliar clients. Third, the means of success must seem at least learnable by other community members. Inspired by the profits, others must be able to plan out their own way forward. At each stage, despite the anomalous nature of some payoffs, the route to success has seemed clear, doable, and replicable to those starting out.

Fourth, the resulting competition does not eliminate producers, and in fact the winner-take-all tournament sustains them. This is abundantly evident for the Tiguans—the most successful intermediaries must recruit and pay part-time painters in order to keep their own earnings high. The less successful painters do not entirely disappear, and since their skill set is really not so different from that of the more successful painters and intermediaries, even a marginal involvement in the craft sustains hope of hitting the big time.

Finally, not only are the big winners unable to detach from the community, they widen their obligations and become anchors of community life. For Tiguans, this materialized as a need to gain legitimacy through a vital link back to Tigua—both for their folk art and for their own standing among their peers from the rural valley. Through their spending, they invested in traditional fiestas, intensified and extended compadre ties, and made their homes in the city into hubs where migrants could again experience a Quichua world. While such spending hardly counts as redistributive, it nevertheless involves the successful painters in the stressful work of reconciling winner-take-all rewards with an ethos of community. Indeed, not only does the ceaseless play for position engender community, it can push a kind of conformity. The anti-resellers in Tigua were especially vocal about this. By chasing the rewards embodied in the designs and practices of the top artisans, small producers shortchanged their own creativity. This leads to the crucial question addressed in the following chapter: as artisan economies are caught up in a rush of expansion, mechanization, and ever-narrower specialization, how does innovation occur?

4

Information-Age Indian Market: Innovation in Moderation

In May 2001, the indigenous artisan Luis Ramos laid off his last three employees, shut down his workshop, and began to make informal inquiries about selling his industrial sewing machines, his mechanical overlocks, and his power knitters. Ramos had been among the pioneers of acrylic sweater manufacture in Otavalo. Ramos played his part in the expansion of local handicraft production into a $15 million-a-year international trade in the mid-1990s (Meisch 2002). Ever-increasing investments coupled with production and design innovation seem destined to take Ramos to the next level—out of artisan manufacture and into the world of industrial entrepreneurs.

A host of problems had set in by the end of the decade: overproduction, currency shocks, and competition from Peru, Thailand, and Nepal. But if Ramos's decline stemmed from these systemic problems, he blamed his fall on the open-air marketplace located a block away from his workshop. He had created a best-selling design, but it was aggressively copied and sold everywhere in Otavalo's Plaza de Ponchos. That same season Ramos's business went bankrupt.

Describing his design, Ramos said it was "the Indian of the

past, our ancestors." He developed it from a historical engraving of an indigenous warrior. With photocopied enlargements, he created a simplified portrait of a stern face, long hair, thick ear plugs, and a feathered headdress. He transferred his design into an array of "Xs" on graph paper and then paid a software programmer in Quito to code it for his knitting machines. After a trial run, Ramos reworked the design, returned to the programmer, and spent another $250 for a version to accommodate a front zipper (see figure 16). Ramos then put the double-faced version into production, creating an icon that became known as the *cara del indio*: the "face of the Indian."

Knowing the risk of copying, Ramos first tried to export sweaters directly to Europe, bypassing any interaction with Ecuadorian marketplace vendors. While trying to line up a sale, two intermediaries came by his shop and bought a sample. Ramos asked them to keep it secret. Nonetheless, about two weeks later,

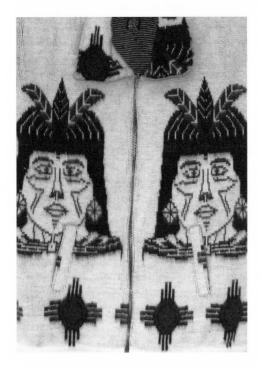

FIGURE 16. Face of the Indian (Photo: Rudi Colloredo-Mansfeld)

Ramos said he saw "a perfect copy" in the display window of a competitor. Soon Ramos quit the business. The design kept spreading, becoming a standard item for Otavalo market stalls and beyond.

Otavalo is full of similar stories of predatory copying—what producers call disloyal competition. These stories follow a simple script. In order to foreshadow the results of a design study presented later in this chapter, we have taken out a sharpie and a piece of graph paper to offer here an illustrated account of this tale, which could be called the myth of the copied design (see figure 17). It starts with a trade of thirty producers who have their operations centered on a market plaza (figure 17a). Through her own creative effort, vendor 4 revamps the star design into something stylishly new (figure 17b). She displays it in the plaza to attract customers and book some new sales (figure 17c). Over the next month, vendor 15 thinks that vendor 4 is onto something. He develops his version and becomes the second person in the plaza with a star design (figure 17d). Having seen vendor 15's

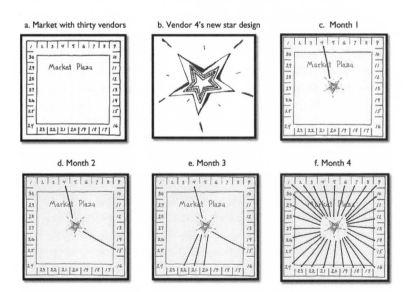

FIGURE 17. The myth of the copied design

success with the design, vendors 20, 21, and 22 rush to get their version out (figure 17e). They, too, find willing customers. By now, everyone knows that the star sells, and they do not want to be left out. By the fourth month, everyone brings a star to market (figure 17f). When it comes to innovation, the meaning of this myth for most Otavaleños is as plain as the star. As a sweater maker put it, "we cannot increase our designs because of the competition and the copying."

Innovation, Copying, and the Commons in an Artisan Market Plaza

Ramos's story returns us to the core issue of innovation in artisan economies. As discussed in the prologue, there is currently an enormous emphasis on innovation, including its prominent role in both the Ecuadorian and Colombian government plans for development and as a focus for corporations and institutions around the world. Ramos exemplifies a line of argument insisting that people will not innovate without patent protection and intellectual property rights. In a market plaza where everything is on display, copying is too easy, and there is no reward for the long toil of innovation. However, a countering line of argument has been to emphasize how sharing and copying can both fuel more innovation and become a sustainable commons resource. In this reasoning, innovation is not simply the result of individual tinkering, but draws from relationships and can replenish a traditional resource base.

This chapter tracks real data on the spread of design innovations in the Otavalo Plaza de Ponchos. With the help of keen-eyed research assistants who kept careful records of design details, we discover that even in a market where there are no patent protections and few secrets, design innovations do not spread indiscriminately. Successful innovations do proliferate, but at an even pace, and with ample room for idiosyncrasies. As one group embraced a new design, another subset continued with an earlier innovation, while nearly all stuck with at least one of the original decorative styles of hand embroidery. This kind of balanced innovation, or innovation-in-moderation, materializes a marketplace as a commons resource. Interestingly, however, this commons resource was built not on cooperation but on suspicion and accusations of cut-throat copy-cat competition.

With the details of Otavalo's market in mind, our first goal is to show that unregulated innovative ideas are not "free," in the sense that they rarely conform to the logic of rapid diffusion, exploitation, and obsolescence in an open market. Our second goal is to account for the documented patterns, and this leads us to observations about the structuring of a commodity's value. The following section begins a discussion of the artisan commodity, investigating the differences and overlap between artisan products and claims about a new information economy. We review the results of an eighteen-month effort to track patterns of innovation and copying among the makers of embroidered cotton shirts. We then return to Luis Ramos's acrylic sweater trade to examine in more detail what producers had to say about their own designs, including opinions on which ones they liked and which ones they did not. The chapter concludes with observations concerning the commons of value that sustains artisan trade.

In the end, it was probably not the copying that bankrupted Ramos as much as a lack of balance in his own enterprise. Ramos was too dependent on catching off-the-street customers and had too few in his network of regular clients. In effect, Ramos had taken a risk to come up with "the big new thing" that would spring him to the top of the heap by offering the most sought-after item. His case is tragic, but not for the fact that he actually came up with the killer new design and could not capitalize on it. (As discussed in the previous chapter, winner-take-all rewards are often not monopolized by the innovators.) It was a tragedy because his failure was foreknown: any sweater producer in Otavalo would guess that the big new design would transform the look of the plaza as a whole far more readily than the fortunes of an individual producer.

Towards a Theory of the Information-Rich Commodity

To understand the business of designing for a native, Andean handicraft trade, it is useful to turn to a radically different economy: the Internet commerce launched in the 1990s. As entrepreneurs raced to reinvent cultural and economic goods for trade on the World Wide Web, economists and business consultants rethought what was actually bought and sold when money was exchanged for a product. These insights coalesced into a set of propositions about commodities in markets that are both global and wired, perhaps best expressed in Philip Evans and Thomas Wurster's *Blown to Bits* (2000).

Evans and Wurster first propose that any object can be disaggregated into its material and intellectual content. Further, "the pure economics of a physical thing and the pure economics of a piece of information are fundamentally different. When a thing is sold, the seller ceases to own it; when an idea, a tune or a blueprint is sold, the seller still possesses it and could possibly sell it again" (2000, 15). Second, much of the value of a good lies in its informational content. Indeed, in a market like Otavalo's Plaza de Ponchos, such a commodity becomes profitable to the extent that it carries enough information in order to accomplish some or all of the following tasks: establish its function and look (its character), associate it with others from the same producer while differentiating it from rivals (its brand), establish its currency and freshness (its fashion), and link it to the traditions of a place and people (its heritage). To illustrate all this, it is worth returning to Ramos's product. As an object, it was two pounds of acrylic fiber, a stainless steel zipper, a nylon label. As information, the item needed enough stylistic cues so that the garment could be considered a "contemporary," "indigenous," "sweater," and from the company "Tejidos Ramos."

A third and important point is how digitizing and electronic connectivity have "broken the link between physical and information economics" (Evans and Wurster 2000, 18). Design, image, and identity can be bought, sold, and lost independently of any physical object. Thus, producers find their business options limited. Evans and Wurster claim that for higher earnings, producers can try to monopolize their ideas either through intellectual property rights or through informal mechanisms such as secrecy; or they can disseminate ideas through licenses or other contracts and earn money from fees. Failing this, if producers lose control of an idea, they must then earn money as a commodity manufacturer selling an interchangeable product. Because of the meager earnings from such production, Evans and Wurster insist that "unless the originators of information have some ability to limit access to others . . . they will never earn a return to justify the original investment" (2000, 15). Put simply, as the economics of information comes to dominate the value of a commodity, producers do best by broadening the reach of their ideas and securing their rights as authors.

Yet a "pure economics of information" embeds a shared political commitment inside an individualized market transaction. The legal scholar Lawrence Lessig (2001; 2004) has pointed out that the freedom of digital ideas and commerce has been constructed in a peculiar way and has melded a market with a commons. Lessig observes that programmers shaped the Internet as a platform that was open, versatile, and simplified. The central architecture is so unspecialized that it can be used for diverse tasks such as transmitting a medical X-ray, exchanging music, or playing on-line poker. Consequently, the economic value of Internet-borne products has largely, but not entirely, been pushed out of the medium of connection—which is shared and standardized—and into the applications that users devise. Far from being natural or inevitable, this structuring of value represents an explicit commitment to openness and defense of a shared system by programmers.[1] The freedom of ideas that allows individuals to profit from a "pure economics for pieces of information" feeds off this artfully made, collective environment. The reach of ideas requires an implicit investment in maintaining a shared human-built architecture of exchange. Freedom is the fruit of assuming the duties of good digital citizenship.

These propositions about value and information and interdependence both extend and invert classic understandings of the commodity. Drawing on Marx, a commodity has conventionally been defined as an object with an exchange value (established when transacted) and a use value (realized by the consumer). Information-rich products add to these an "idea value" that transcends any single object and serves to organize market categories, rivalry among enterprises, and opportunities for participation. Yet for all the transcendence of the idea value, it too is an object whose equivalence can be established with other objects. In social terms, a classic commodity is fully alienated—stripped of any connection to the producer—at the moment of exchange. Information-rich commodities, though, are hybrids: the physical good is alienated, handed over to the buyer; the design and image remains connected to the seller; and the elements that facilitated transmission are beholden to the collective that established the infrastructure of exchange.

On the face of it, an indigenous textile economy with pre-Incan roots in the northern Andes seems the precise opposite of the Internet-based economy that was launched with Silicon Valley venture capital in the 1990s. Yet Evans and Wurster's succinct description of the risks and rewards of information economics captures Luis Ramos's experience. And the analogies are not purely coincidental. Artisans in Otavalo have not only mechanized their production, they have invested in computer technology that simplifies designs and multiplies their availability. Indeed, textile goods have long had a programmable quality, with designs that involve mathematical progressions, codified representations, and interchangeable application within a standard technical base. In 1994, when interviewed about their design innovations, belt weavers in Ariasucu referred to notebooks of graph paper to demonstrate variations in the warp patterns they made on wooden treadle looms (see chapter 3).

The rapid spread of the "face of the Indian" design across the Plaza de Ponchos illustrates how quickly ideas can travel now that producers have so simplified the fiber, fabric, and tailoring of their products. They have made of the acrylic sweater in particular a generic textile screen across which the designs conjured and stored on their laptops and flash drives appear. Or to switch metaphors, they have created the perfect medium to support an invasive new design and allowed it to propagate rapidly. Of all the goods in Otavalo, these sweaters come closest to supporting the myth of the copied design.

Public Life of Shirt Designs

In 2001, when we began investigating patterns of innovation, we found that imitation did not bother everyone. To be sure, during interviews with twenty-one manufacturers of acrylic sweaters in 2001, about half complained of rivals who priced goods unfairly, or sent someone to their showrooms to buy a sample under false pretenses, or "spied on their shop windows from the street corner." Other producers, though, were accustomed to these issues and saw them as routine. As one woman put it, she copies and others copy her: "Everyone copies. We are not selfish. It is a free market." Another woman explained that quick turnover in designs caused her to get a programmable knitting machine so she could keep up with other producers. Still another producer reported that market woes had united everyone, saying "I know what the others are doing. I talk to them and ask. No one is selling. It is not the competition. When one is able to sell, all are able to sell." If for some copying is to blame for every ill, for others copying is a reassuring sign of connection.[2]

In 2006, we set out to document how producers displayed their designs to attract customers. We wanted to know how much overlap existed in their public inventories and how quickly design innovations actually spread. We focused on cotton shirt makers for several reasons. First, their business involved between fifty and sixty regular producers, offering a relatively broad sample to observe. Shirt makers also shared with the sweater makers an increasing investment in computerized designs as they began to purchase new embroidering machines that had programmable settings.

The study involved publicly displayed innovations, and could not always capture all the new designs developed by producers. Nonetheless, the gap between the innovation that was out for display and more private forms did not seem to be large. Some producers who registered high sales and offered diverse displays reported they were indifferent to copies and usually displayed samples from their latest production runs. Others did try to keep designs secret and export them directly, but they complained that intermediaries still would buy samples abroad and send them back for rivals to copy and display. Still others did have exclusive designs, but they reported that these were often special motifs designed by an international client for a particular market or event and were not something that the producer would sell again.

More than that, we wanted to focus on display because even within Otavalo many producers considered the Plaza de Ponchos to be the real problem, an epicenter of rapid copies and minimal innovation. As one store owner described his contempt of the plaza: "My designs are original because I manufacture a high quality product, which I put a high value on and give different prices than in the market plaza. In contrast, the vendors make mistakes on the sizes of their goods and the poor quality of their raw material leads them to lower their price without earning any kind of profit."

We therefore divided the sample to include fifteen vendors who sold in the open Plaza de Ponchos and fifteen vendors who sold through their own stores in the neighborhood around the plaza. Based on research begun in 2004 on shirt designs, we created a checklist of thirteen details to track across all producers. The elements represented a cross-section of creative sources: artisan textiles such as "Inca" cloth appliqué; local, indigenous Otavaleña blouse fashion details such as sequins; and women's fashion from other Ecuadorian indigenous groups, such as hand embroidery of Zuleta. These details varied in the technology and skill producers needed. Switching from embroidery to appliqué, for example, could require reworking a technique or finding a new skilled piece worker to employ. Beginning in May 2006 and finishing in December 2007, we spot checked the thirty producers once a month.

Over those eighteen months, the cotton shirt trade had no "star fashion" moment. That is, there was no sudden widespread adoption of some hot new design. Rather, hand embroidery, which was the original adornment of these shirts, proved ubiquitous. Month after month, all but two or three of our thirty producers displayed shirts with flowers and curlicues stitched by hand (see figure 18).[3]

Thus our first observation of display practices: contemporary artisans work to establish their commonality with each other before they differentiate themselves. If this seems obvious, modern business strategy assumes the opposite. Conventional wisdom holds that a firm must differentiate itself from its rivals and then capture the value of that difference. And by extension, the economics of information reinforces notions that exclusive ideas are the ones that deliver value. Certainly, many Otavaleños pursue this value by inventing new designs and trying to keep them secret. Yet on their hangers and mannequins, they show off the stitched flowers and other motifs that replicate their neighbors' display. Their collective display makes puffy-sleeved, embroidered shirts a coherent and predictable artisan commodity.

A second observation: just because a detail has a previous history of circulation and has ties to indigenous culture does not mean it will be preserved. As with embroidery, sequins had been a popular feature on indigenous women's own blouses. Yet over the course of the study, they went out of style and became hard to find (see figure 19).

Third, producers differentiated themselves with a show of their wares, primarily through the quantity of designs. Producers generally fit into one of three categories. Many stick with a small set of the usual embroidered motifs. A second type of operator likewise puts up these bread-and-butter styles, but then specializes in some additional feature, whether appliqué or Amazonian

FIGURE 18. Month-to-month count of firms displaying an item with hand embroidery

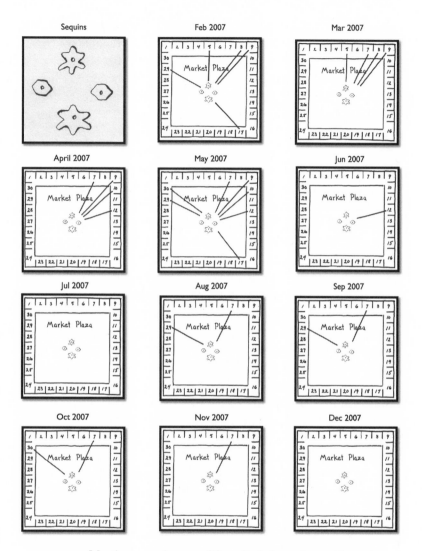

FIGURE 19. Month-to-month count of firms displaying an item with sequins

beads or tie-dyeing. A corollary of such specialization was that certain design elements only partially spread in the market (see figure 20). Inca cloth appliqué, for example, neither went out of style nor went on to become a signature style for the cotton shirts. The third group broadly diversifies their designs to cover the full range of market fashions. Interestingly, "design-rich" firms were not necessarily cash-rich firms. Using the number of employees as a proxy for firm revenue, we did not find a correlation between workforce size and the number of details that producers put on display. It was true that producers with a store, which generally signifies a more capitalized operation, did show on average about three more design elements than those with only market posts. Yet of all thirty producers, the second most prolific displayer was a vendor in the Plaza de Ponchos.[4]

Finally, among our thirty producers over the eighteen months, we noted just four innovations, and of these, three were limited to just a few producers. Not surprisingly, even singling out a change in the shirts as an innovation was a methodological challenge. To offer a hypothetical case: if a producer displays shirts in which the same hand-embroidered flowers are done exclusively in black thread, does it constitute a new detail (because no one had used black before) or continuity (because it was a color variation of hand embroidery, a detail that has a range of color variations to begin with)? Designs were tweaked here and there, but did such alterations matter?

An innovation is more than novelty, it is a "difference that makes a difference" to borrow an influential phrasing from Gregory Bateson (1972, 459). For our research assistants, who not only were experienced investigators but also had been involved in the shirt business, such differences-that-make-a-difference only became practical to track once they were copied and could be verbally identified by the artisans themselves. Thus, one of the innovations we observed was a variant of computerized embroidery that had been modeled on President Rafael Correa's inaugural shirt first seen by the public in January 2007. When knockoffs began to be sold later that winter, they were first noted

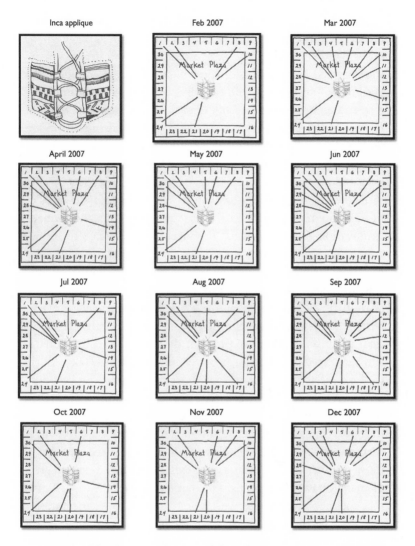

FIGURE 20. Month-to-month count of firms displaying an item with "Inca" cloth appliqué

in the study within an existing category as "computerized embroidery," although the motifs were about four times bigger than other such embroidery. By June, producers all referred to a new standardized composition of these panels of large embroidered designs as "presidential" and our observers began recording it as a separate adornment (see figure 21). Of the four innovations, the presidential embroidery showed signs of growing adoption, with eleven different producers creating a version by the end of the year. Yet even the taking up of this sellable new feature was slow and incremental.

Eighteen months of observation indicated that the public life of designs in the plaza fit a pattern that could be termed "innovation-in-moderation." Producers did continue to innovate, hanging out shirts with brand new details, embellishing traditional techniques, and renovating their market displays. But it is "in moderation" because this activity represents a small portion of the overall designs in the market. Most producers make a point to display what their neighbors currently offer, and few rush to embrace the novelties that do crop up. Such gradualism may have a practical reason. Many new details take effort to learn; a few cost three or four times more than prior versions of a similar detail. Even so, several producers did say that if they thought a new motif would sell, they would be quick to adopt it. If the shirt makers' steady, low-key innovative activity is not surprising, it does challenge the expectations of a pure economics of information, as well as the expectations and complaints of many Otavaleño artisans. The market showed the capacity to mix openness and copying with innovation and experimentation.

Fashion, Culture, and Value

The blending of imitation and innovation has recently been explored in work on intellectual property rights, especially for apparel industries (Barrère and Delabruyère 2011). These links rest on the logic of fashion, as explored in Georg Simmel's classic reflections (1997, 189). By continually updating the goods that

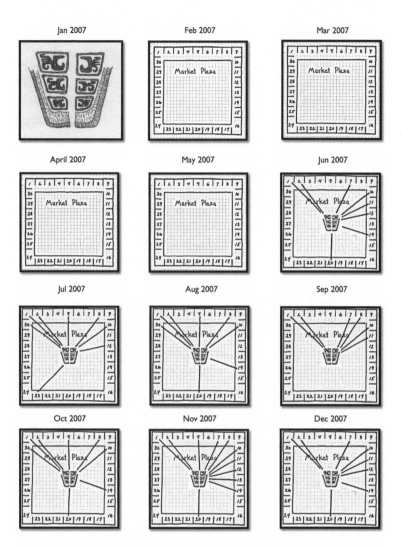

FIGURE 21. Month-to-month count of firms displaying an item with "presidential" embroidery

let individuals fit in with a desirable social class and break away from social inferiors, apparel makers drive fashion onwards and thereby profit from rapid product cycles. Yet they only earn if their novel designs serve the social aspirations of consumers, and they can only do that by fitting the trend. Individually, copying limits a single designer's risk of being left out. Collectively, mutual imitation serves all designers: "Copying helps to anchor the new season to a limited number of design themes, which are freely workable by all firms in the industry" (Raustiala and Sprigman 2006, 1729). Put another way, when it comes to clothes, the economics of information entails key positive externalities. As long as producers enjoy the freedom to replicate, abandon, and imitate anew, then their private actions achieve the public benefit of a profitable trend. They establish a tangible market segment with a "fashion value" that allows all to earn a premium.

In Otavalo, though, fashion is not the only force shaping the economics of imitation. Shirt makers and other artisans aim to create a product with "identity" that conveys the heritage of the Quichua people of the region. In contrast to both fashion and to individual artistry, cultural items are the ones that resist ephemeral change and stand apart from a producer's personal aesthetic (Eglash 1999). The cultural ideas conserve a group ethos, running "through the social fabric" to organize collective representations and exhibit a shared identity through time (Eglash 1999, 39). Here again conformity can generate value, but the logic of heritage runs counter to that of trendiness.

We wanted to know whether Otavaleño producers recognized a split between fashion and heritage in their wares—and whether they linked traditions to earnings. We also wanted to find out about producer aesthetics in order to establish an individual artistic vision, such as that of Luis Ramos, as a source of value. To raise fashion as a more explicit concern, we expanded the sample to include Atuntaqui, the neighboring town that produces casual wear for the national market and prides itself on its fashion sense. The sample was structured to include three trades that varied in the locally marked cultural traditions associated with their goods: (1) Atuntaqui, mestizo acrylic sweater makers specializing in styles taken from international retail websites; (2) Otavalo, indigenous acrylic sweater makers specializing in knitted garments that date back only fourteen years; and (3) Otavalo, indigenous shirt makers specializing in a garment that has roots in both traditional men's clothing and women's embroidery (see the prologue).

To solicit opinions about the cultural relevance of current commodity designs, we used photographs of twenty items from each trade and worked with men and women who had principle design responsibility for their workshop.[5] Designers rated the fashion of each item on a scale from one to five (the Spanish phrase *de la moda*, in fashion, captured both the idea of trendiness and salability). They rated their own preference for each item and scored the cultural significance of each one. We phrased the cultural significance question as "how much does this item represent the identity of Otavalo (or Atuntaqui)?" to avoid a narrow idea of folklore that the term "culture" connotes and that tripped up Atuntaqui producers.

The study began in Atuntaqui but unfortunately had to be discontinued because the annual summer trade show demanded the attention of the producers. Initial results with eleven respondents suggested a close relationship between fashion and preference that we expected in a market of casual wear. A hooded, broadly striped sweater received both the highest average fashion score and the highest average personal preference score. Likewise, a shorter black-trimmed sweater with a scalloped waist received the lowest fashion score and the lowest preference score. Meanwhile, the producers struggled with the question, "Does this item represent the identity of Atuntaqui?" Some offered uniformly high ratings and others rated each item uniformly low—the overall average was in the middle, but this was a result of answers either at the low or high end of the scale.

In Otavalo, we reached fifteen out of the seventeen producers of acrylic sweaters and forty-one of the forty-two shirt producers who at that time regularly sold in the Wednesday or Saturday markets. The most consistent difference between the two Otavalo trades was a business practice. Shirt makers were more likely to sell in the Plaza de Ponchos. Twenty of them had market stalls, fifteen had stand-alone stores, and five sold through both market stalls and stores. In contrast, all fifteen of the sweater makers had their own stores, with only two producers also selling in the market. Indeed, most sweater makers took a dim view of the Plaza de Ponchos, condemning it for its lack of quality products.

On the whole, sweater makers were not impressed by their own offerings. We sorted these proprietors into groups according to the three scales. Those whose average ranking for all twenty items fell at the low end (below 3.0 on the five-point scale) for the three different measures we labeled as "fashion skeptics," "generally not liking," and "cultural skeptics." Those whose average rankings were over 3.0 we placed in categories of "fashion backer," "generally liking," and "cultural backer." By this standard, sweater makers dismissed most of their products. By nearly a 3-to-1 ratio, they generally did not like their products, saw little cultural value in them, and were even less convinced they were fashionable.

Across their answers, sweater makers revealed that their hearts were not with culture, but fashion. In scoring their own products' fashion and identity, the sweater makers clearly distinguished among those goods that represented indigenous Otavalo culture, such as the face of the Indian, and those that did not, such as a panda bear. Not surprisingly, sweaters that were highest in cultural value were seen to be among the least fashionable. Although the negative relationship between culture and fashion was not statistically significant for all twenty articles, the five most culture-worthy designs included three of the lowest fashion scores (see figure 22, items 9, 10, 11). Yet if fashion diverged from cultural ratings, it tracked personal preferences very tightly.[6] Producers preferred goods that stood at the profitable edge of current trends. In sum, producers believed that sweaters could bear cultural imagery, but those sweaters did not follow market trends. Rarely, however, did the sweaters exhibit much cultural

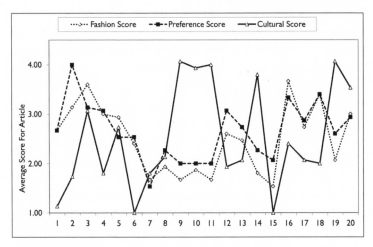

FIGURE 22. Comparison of cultural, fashion, and preference scores of twenty acrylic sweater designs

value in the eyes of their makers—and, more damning, even less fashion. Sweater producers seemed to have sunk into an innovation and design malaise.

Shirt makers were more upbeat. Their scores for personal preference tended to be higher, with the average of their means at 3.06 as compared to 2.65 for the sweater makers.[7] Average cultural scores tended to be higher as well, with an average cultural rating of 2.9 compared to the sweater makers' 2.5 cultural rating average.[8] In terms of fashion, a small majority of shirt makers saw the shirts they made as fashionable (twenty-four cases) as compared to the seventeen cases that fell into the "fashion skeptic" category. Indeed, using the same values to group shirt makers as was used to group the sweater makers, we found that they split more closely down the middle, with a much wider variance on all three scales. However, despite this variance, shirt makers shared with their sweater-making neighbors a preference for fashionable items, though the correlation was not as tight.[9]

In an effort to gain another perspective on the cultural ratings and design preferences of the sweater makers, we repeated the interviews using the same selection of designs but with a group of students at the University of Iowa. The tastes of college undergraduates are particularly relevant because they make up a significant portion of Otavalo's target market. Students enrolled in "Latin American Economy and Society" were selected for their basic awareness of the circumstances of artisan production in South America. That is, they understood the category of good they were being asked to rate. Among the twenty-nine respondents, though, none had visited or read about Otavalo.

As with the sweater makers, the items that students preferred correlated with what they considered fashionable.[10] However, what students liked and what they judged to be trendy did not match up at all with what the sweater makers liked or what they saw as fashionable. The correlation between average fashion scores provided by undergraduates in Iowa and artisans in Otavalo was .100, and of preference .023. Judgment of the cultural value of products, though, proved to be altogether different. When it came to picking out which of the twenty items represented Otavalo identity and which did not, student ratings correlated highly with the producers ($.858, p < .01$) despite the lack of direct knowledge about the place and its people. Whatever else it is, the "native Andeanness" represented by those sweaters clearly entails a particular point of intersection between Iowa college students and Otavaleño artisans, a point we now address in more detail.

Designs, Trends, and Place

The preference survey explored whether a cultural aesthetic offered a special source of value for Otavalo textile producers. Participants in both Otavalo trades did in fact identify cultural details that stood apart from the market's fashion trends. Yet producers were divided over what money, if any, was to be made from these elements. Many shirt makers viewed their designs positively in terms of both sales and cultural integrity. Sweater makers struggled to find anything good to say.

Here is one of the ironies that befell sweater makers: Worried about the copying and underhanded selling they said takes place in the plaza, they retreated to their own stores. Yet such isolation delivered neither aesthetic nor economic rewards. In 2004, they had tired of their designs. In a follow-up economic survey in 2005, we found that three of the fifteen surveyed firms had shut their stores. In contrast, all forty-two cotton shirt-making businesses were still operating. Further, we discovered new shirt-making enterprises that had started up within the previous year. Whatever damage is done by the mutual theft of design ideas in the plaza, it did not apparently undermine the overall sustainability of the shirt trade.

There is a deeper puzzle to the sweater makers' discontent. If the producers do not like these sweaters, and if buyers no longer seem interested in them, and if they have a history that is in fact only a few years old, why do producers continue to make them? At one level, producers are trying to live up to a stereotype of "native handicrafts." The matching of the Iowa and Otavalo culture scales indicates a broadly shared vision of what counts as native. Put another way, the criteria for establishing the indigenousness of some Otavalo products are not specific to Otavalo's own Plaza de Ponchos. Quite the opposite—the Plaza de Ponchos itself is better seen as a product of these criteria. Ideas about indigenous crafts shared in Iowa and Otavalo stem from related, shared concepts of the traditional, the native, and the less developed. The quest for such premodern authenticity sets in motion the travel and purchasing that gives rise to marketplaces like that in Otavalo. Producers must satisfy these longings, and a knitted llama motif was a solution in the early 2000s.

This explanation, however, comes with a built-in contradiction. While it is tempting to attribute these tired designs to the trap of selling "native handicrafts," Otavaleños have no more been held by this trap than they have been stuck in their corn fields on the side of Mount Imbabura. Their artisan practices remain fluid and creative. To note the obvious: the very fact that they manufacture acrylic sweaters with fifty different programmable designs indicates a shift in the boundaries of native goods. Moreover, they are business people, happy to produce stale designs if they sell and ready to abandon them if they do not. In light of this creativity and business rationality, the staying power of the low-selling llamas remains a problem.

The solution to the puzzle may well be, once again, found in the physical Plaza de Ponchos. Indeed, a spot-observation census of sweater designs displayed in Otavalo in 2005 showed a strong relationship between the plaza and culturally related designs. In the shop windows of the producers, only 6 percent of the units (2 of 33 sweaters) exhibited llamas. Out in the plaza—a segment of the market that received less than 1 percent of producers' sales in a 2001 survey—82 percent of the displayed sweaters (268 of 325) featured llamas. That is, while explicitly Andean designs sold at much lower rates, the Plaza de Ponchos market vendors displayed them at much higher rates. These commodities seem to have a value that is specifically tied to their use as items for display. Indeed, for the vendor, surrounded by Che Guevara T-shirts, manufactured hammocks, and plain woolen sweaters, the llama patterns may be the only item that proclaims the native identity of the wares.

These cultural designs are not to be taken in isolation, but rather as contextual cues that lead observers to interpret whole sets of products as native. Collectively, such commodities shape the future of the market square. Since the mid-twentieth century, the Plaza de Ponchos has developed as a powerful, open platform of exchange. Physically, it is austere, an empty city block paved in cement, demarcated by white lines into hundreds of market stalls. The value is not in this architecture, which is open, simple, and basic, but in the interactivity of tourists and artisans who bring an Indian market to life. Garments that serve in any given moment as indigenous emblems simultaneously draw from and contribute to the indigeneity of this whole mode of exchange.

Peasant and Artisan Markets: Not Blown to Bits

Just down the street from Otavalo's Plaza de Ponchos is a peasant market, stuffed with agricultural goods and the cheap items that the nontourists buy. Otavalo's peasant market has been there longer than the Plaza de Ponchos, like the peasant markets in Zumbagua that serve Tiguan communities, which predate the rise of Tigua art, and the persistent peasant market in the middle of all those new casual-wear mall stores in fashionable Atuntaqui (see chapter 5).

Throughout the northern Andes, the elites tend to treat these peasant markets with scorn and embarrassment. Elites typically portray peasant markets as relics from an earlier era, and they hope they can be eliminated by a modern supermarket, or perhaps legislated out of existence. When the provincial capital of Pasto, Colombia, inaugurated a new bus terminal, the regional newspaper asked *¿Hasta Cuando?*, Until When? encapsulating elite feeling about the peasant market nearby: "The disorder of the market is a constant . . . at only 200 meters from the modern transport terminal which is for showing off, we have a market that should be hidden from visitors" (*Diario del Sur* October 16, 1996, 7a; Antrosio 2008, chap. 6).

For elites, the peasant market embodies disorder, an atavistic chaos. The story of Túquerres, the peasant-marketing town discussed in chapter 2, is in part about the struggles to relocate vendors into market stalls at the edge of the city. It seemed that every year, announcements were made about an impending reorganization, about how the town would finally be cracking down on informal vendors. Yet even after the rise and fall of the financial pyramids, the oldest and most central marketplace was still staffed with vendors.

These markets endure. The peasant marketplace has likely been a feature of peasant agricultural production for centuries (see chapter 2). The artisan producers and traders of the northern Andes almost certainly learned lessons about marketing from these marketplaces. However, these marketplaces are far from being unchanged relics. Vendors now sell knit Chinese imports, pirated DVDs, and cell phones, mixed in with hybrid potato varieties, cabbages, and carrots, often grown with lots of chemical fertilizers and pesticides. The peasant marketplace is perhaps the original source for the innovation-in-moderation observed in the artisan Plaza de Ponchos.

A related point is that peasant markets and informal vendors have almost never been threatened by purely economic forces. There have been many attempts to legislate, police, and bully the markets out of existence (Seligmann 2004), but there has hardly ever been a case in which a supermarket or other industry was so modern and efficient that the informal marketing disappeared. Quite the opposite—as urban centers have grown, so have the agricultural markets to service them. This occurs even when a vendor seems to be doing not much more than breaking down a five-pound bag of sugar into one-pound packets. Meager earnings, yes, but enough to keep on trading. Like the artisan vendors who strive to successfully copy others before differentiating, there is something to be gained from trading in reliable, known quantities.

Like the Plaza de Ponchos, the peasant marketplaces, with their stalls, bargaining, and supply-and-demand price swings, are all materialized by the vendors themselves. Although the larger towns typically have dedicated market buildings, smaller towns continue a weekly rotating market tradition in a designated area that may be only a field or empty lot. In the predawn hours, vendors and hired porters bring in the entire apparatus, like a traveling performance. They are competing, yet they are in a crucial relationship of community, and without each person contributing individually the very value of the commodities for sale falls into jeopardy.

These observations enable us to return to the ideas in Evans and Wurster's *Blown to Bits*. Published in early 2000, the technology-heavy NASDAQ index was rapidly rising, topping 5,000 in March 2000. It seemed that the pure economics of information had crossed a new threshold of wealth generation. Of course, then the NASDAQ crashed. As of mid-2014 the NASDAQ was around 4,500, still about 10 percent off its peak after fourteen years. *Blown to Bits* is full of stories of disintermediation and transformation, but the very companies doing the disintermediation would soon suffer traditional blow-ups and burnouts. This is not to say that everything returned to stable bedrock. Indeed, the ongoing lesson of *Blown to Bits* has been instability everywhere, that the disruptive innovators—to return to Clayton Christensen (1997)—will themselves soon be disrupted. Nevertheless, the peasant and artisan markets provide some lessons in durability—individual vendors and trades come and go, yet the materialized market and the economics of physical things endures.

What Evans and Wurster's argument missed is that information, product, place, and labor process can still coalesce in powerful ways. These aspects may be vulnerable to disaggregation, but they are also susceptible to reaggregation. What once were apparently completely standardized commodities, like one-pound bags of coffee, have been reimagined with artisan place and artisan labor. Indeed, fair-trade coffee captures its premium precisely for the way the thing and the information—the coffee bean and the story of the farm that produced it—now can become fused (Lyon 2011).

To return to the discussion of the economics of information offered at the beginning of the chapter, Otavalo's textile designs reflect the layers of value that commodities gain from information. For the producer, a sweater earns something for being a utilitarian object, something more for being a native craft, and still again more profit when a buyer finds a design to be unique and unavailable in other garments. The value in play not only has different sources, but a transaction transforms that value into different kinds of resources. The sale of a sweater in the plaza leaves the buyer in exclusive possession of a brand new article of clothing to dispose of as he or she sees fit. The producer retains a potentially profitable idea to resell to others. The plaza, too, gains in the process of the sale. A category of craft good, the work of market stall commerce, and the fame of Otavalo indigenous textiles all are renewed as components of viable livelihood when buyer and seller exchange a commodity that both accept as indigenous.

Economists often label such aspects "externalities," as if they were peripheral to the real business of buying and selling. Such a term is misleading, as it understates and misplaces the shared value at stake. For Otavaleños, all these side effects of exchange can be *internal*, both to an artisan's enterprise and to an artisan sense of self. Handicrafts, market sales, and textile know-how are precisely what artisans and vendors talk about when defending an "economy with identity"—a term producers have been using since the 1980s to defend the livelihood of artisans on the plaza. To put it more strictly in terms of a commodity, the marginal sales value that shop-worn, stereotyped Andean motifs offer is inextricably coupled with a durable base value. This deep value sustains the intelligibility, meaning, and activity that make an open market for native textiles possible.

It is in this way that although artisan economies can involve a great deal of risk, and have in the last few decades spread as invasive trades with winner-take-all dynamics, they can nevertheless be powerfully routinized. The invasive trade can become managed within older patterns of innovation-in-moderation, another resource for the historically invaded community. In fact, although national elites deride or ignore the innovative capacities of peasants and artisans, the lessons learned from market plazas in the northern Andes can be just as potent as advice shared from the management consultants of *Blown to Bits* or from the business gurus from *The Innovator's DNA* (Dyer, Gregersen, and Christensen 2011). The story of what happens when consultants meet artisans is found in the next chapter.

5

Artisan Public Economies and Cluster Development

In 2001, a small group of clothing manufacturers launched a new trade show called Expoferia in the Ecuadorian town of Atuntaqui. Elsewhere in Ecuador, the manufacturing sector was reeling from the 2000 "dollarization" of the economy. The abandonment of the national currency and associated fiscal reforms were bankrupting hundreds of textile operators, furniture makers, and other small businesses. Producers in Atuntaqui, though, worked with renewed energy. Backed by national television advertising, their Expoferia drew an estimated 20,000 in its first year and grew to attract 100,000 by 2006 (see figure 23). Manufacturers went on a building spree, opening new showrooms along the town's main avenues. Government offices at the local and national levels got on board. Ecuador's consulates issued press reports promoting Atuntaqui's fashion along with the country's better-known bananas and cut flowers. Delegations from other provincial towns came calling on the local Chamber of Commerce, trying to learn the secret of Atuntaqui's turnaround.

What lies behind Atuntaqui's success? When asked in 2005, the mayor responded, "coming together in associations." For his town or any town to get ahead, Mayor Yépez spoke of the "clus-

FIGURE 23. Crowds at Atuntaqui trade show in 2006 (Photo: Angelo Palencia, used by permission)

ter": "How can we successively structure a cluster that brings together however many, one, two, three, ten, twenty-five? The important thing is that we arrive with a better capacity, to create the capacity to build something, to initiate a change in mentality." Many of Atuntaqui's textile shops were officially registered as artisan and were home-based endeavors. Even so, they had come to think of themselves as an industrial cluster poised to compete with much larger rivals in Quito and across the border in Colombia.

The idea of the cluster—and in Atuntaqui they had begun using the English loan-word "cluster," softened a bit with a Hispanicized pronunciation as "clooster"—arrived with international consultants and their PowerPoint presentations. Adopted from Harvard Business School professor, popular business author, and consultant Michael Porter's (1998) ideas of competitiveness in the global economy, the cluster was the rallying cry for a collective commitment to engineering competitive advantage in an age of globalization. Hailing from Central America, Chile, and Colombia, consultants and academics invited T-shirt, sweater, and pajama makers into conference rooms in Atuntaqui's town hall. They explained tactics of strategic cooperation among rivals to achieve a distinctive geographic specialization. While on the one hand Michael Porter's ideas of competitive advantage spurred the work of Clayton Christensen toward a "Gospel of Innovation" (Lepore 2014), Atuntaqui artisans practically translated Porter's ideas of competitive advantage as the need to associate in a cluster.

And the most remarkable thing? It worked. Atuntaqui in 2006 was nothing like Atuntaqui in 1996. Atuntaqui's formerly cloistered home-based textile shops gave way to brightly lit, glass fronted showrooms. In window after window, proprietors taped up signs: "Workers wanted," "Machine Operators wanted," "Salesgirl wanted." Atuntaqui became so successful that other Ecuadorian towns sent emissaries to try and copy the model— Atuntaqui did not just sell clothes, it sold the cluster idea that helped sell the clothes.

This chapter describes what we found when we went to study fashion and production in the mid-2000s in what we thought was a no-name provincial town on the highway heading north from Otavalo. "Success through Clusters" turned out to be just a small episode in a rich history of manufacture, social life, and politics unfolding on Mount Imbabura's western slopes. The cluster explanation was only part of the story—and there were plenty of surprises.

First, Atuntaqui was in the mid-twentieth-century home to one of the largest textile factories in South America, an industrial operation so big that today it is the only one in Ecuador to have official National Heritage status. Atuntaqui had only become a formal township because its manufacturing facility drew so many workers and vendors into its parish. In the 1950s, the air raid siren that announced shift changes at the factory synchronized life throughout the township. Being a factory town meant conditions were already in place for implementing a cluster scheme. Second, despite the huge factory, Atuntaqui was still a small town. The cluster initiative depended on the efforts of a few prominent producers, related by kinship. Two tight-knit sets of siblings and in-laws received the bulk of the benefits from the cluster program. Third, the growth of retail shops accelerated in the 2000s independently of the plans and discussions of the cluster participants. An economic initiative that was once strategic became massively speculative. Fourth, there were cluster initiatives in nearby towns and even within Atuntaqui that did not succeed—the simple idea that clusters solve everything was not supported. Finally, even as the textile cluster itself was succeeding it was creating problems of overproduction, tired designs, and commercial inequalities—unequal access to supposedly joint municipal programs.

In light of the history, social ties, and public debates of Atuntaqui's textile cluster, we argue that one of the town's main lessons lies less in the clustering of similar businesses than in the benefits of transforming a hidden economy into a public economy. Textile production that had been kept behind walls in artisan family workshops went on full display in showrooms and tradeshows. This new public economy took a civic life beyond the consultants' idea of cluster development as social capital. The artisan public economy generated a shared sphere of ideas, discussion, organizing, and civic involvement. As in the previous chapter, market-based competition resulted in economic value—a reputation for fashion, a capacity for large-scale events, a widening pool of skilled workers—that transcended and united individual enterprises. And again, turning to the idea of the commons helps to understand these shared resources and the challenge of governing them. Indeed, for all their efforts to modernize by following contemporary prescriptions for competitive advantage, Atuntaqui proprietors wound up coping with the age-old problems of exploiting, regenerating, and defending a joint asset.

Unlike the artisan producers of Otavalo, the Atuntaqui businesses have little need to ground their products or practices in tradition—they seek only the most fashionable, the modern, the innovative. Moreover, except for possible taxation benefits and legal classifications, there is no reason for a small shop to remain in the artisan sector, as the consumer of casual wear clothing rarely asks (or even wants to know) about labor practices. However, as some successful producers have attempted to exit the artisan sector, the Atuntaqui experiment has faltered. The economy has threatened to retreat behind closed doors—no big public expositions, few joint initiatives, little investment in local brands—and lose collective momentum. The individual abandonment of artisan production has exacted a public price.

From Clusters to Public Economy

From approximately 2000 to 2005, Atuntaqui textile producers operationalized the business theory of the cluster as a series of quality improvement projects. Local leaders solicited help from national ministries who in turn recruited international consultants. The consultants arrived to begin technical changes by cultivating intensive forms of cooperation (Colloredo-Mansfeld and Antrosio 2009; 2012).

In an analysis of this transformation, César Paredes (2010) traced how government programs transformed a preexisting agglomeration of small- and medium-sized textile operations into a nationally identified industrial cluster that was represented by a few larger producers and a national cloth supplier. Paredes addresses four limitations to this cluster approach to development: (1) high levels of exploitation in the primarily female labor force; (2) competition among small firms, which leads to price undercutting rather than product innovation; (3) failure to develop truly complementary industries within the cluster; and (4) the underdevelopment of other economic sectors such as agriculture. Paredes concludes:

> We would be then faced with a clear example of over-specialization, an element that will gravely affect planning processes of local development in the region, putting limits on the process, since if the

economy depends on only one type of industry, the chances of collapse are increased when the textile sector has to face adverse conditions. (2010, 111)

Paredes offers an astute analysis of the negative externalities of the cluster initiative in Atuntaqui (for a more general evaluation see Martin and Sunley 2003).[1] At the same time, however, Paredes underplays what Atuntaqui gained by tying technical change and competitiveness to a program of association among producers. The cultivation of social networks and the insistence on regular open interactions represented a startling commitment to the idea of social capital in development. Such faith manifested in the formation of the Atuntaqui Chamber of Commerce, visits between workshops, municipal planning initiatives, and discussions about textiles as cultural patrimony. Socialized in these settings, economic programs escaped narrow, instrumental limits. Participants took the lessons in economic solidarity with their peers seriously, and recognized the lasting good of staying connected even as one-off projects came and went.

In academic terms, the starting point for most discussions of this connectivity is social capital—the straightforward idea of "friends, colleagues and more general social contacts through whom you receive opportunities to use your financial and human capital" (Burt 1992, 9). Since the 1980s, researchers and development experts have tended to use the idea in two broad ways. The first focuses on the individual and draws lessons from Pierre Bourdieu and others about how a stock of durable relations becomes "usable as a reliable source of other benefits" (Portes 1998, 3). Social capital in this sense magnifies a person's human capital and can be strategically cultivated through specific transactions (Bourdieu 1986). Indeed, investments in education, professional credentials, and other components of human capital will return few benefits unless a person learns to tap the networks that schools and business associations implicitly offer (Coleman 1988).

Alternatively, social capital has been taken to mean the stable and institutionalized relations among a set of actors. Rather than individuals, formal organizations are the locus of analysis. In the United States, Robert Putnam has been at the forefront of this research. At times, he offers an all-encompassing defini- tion: "by 'social capital' I mean features of social life—networks, norms, and trust—that enable participants to act together more effectively to pursue shared objectives" (Putnam 1995, 664–65). Nevertheless, Putnam frequently operationalizes social capital in narrow ways to mean membership in specific groups, such as churches, clubs, unions, and, most famously, bowling leagues. This institutional focus in turn allows him to measure how much social capital a community, region, or nation possesses.

Trumpeting data on declining participation in everything from the Red Cross to garden clubs, Putnam declares that "evidence from a number of independent sources strongly suggests that America's stock of social capital has been shrinking for more than a quarter century" (1995, 666). Scholars and politicians have extensively engaged with and at times criticized Putnam's approach, critiquing the logical circularity (Portes 1998), a simplistic or absent political analysis (Navarro 2002), or a misguided insertion of market-based thinking into social lives and development politics (Fine 2001). Indeed, the debate over social capital itself has prompted its own criticisms for its polemical rhetoric that neglects rigorous local analysis (Bebbington 2004; Roca 2002).

Research in Ecuador thoughtfully bypasses the worst of the debate. It has shown the usefulness of asking questions about the presence of social capital without accepting the insistence on social capital's causal importance (Martínez Valle 2003; Martínez Valle and North 2009). Martínez Valle highlights the conditions that favor sustained relations among small producers in the highlands and how development projects and social linkages mutually reinforce each other. Yet even when Martínez Valle and North dutifully engage theories of social capital, their ambivalence comes through. An insightful chapter asks, "Does social capital exist in Pelileo?" and offers a plausible answer: "No" (Martínez Valle and North 2009).

The problem extends beyond simply trying to identify whether social capital is present. The wider literature on social capital tends to dwell exclusively on the positive: networks of trust, information, and opportunity. It overlooks the well-documented costs of tight social relations, such as the exclusion of outsiders and loss of freedom (Portes 1998). Decades ago, Andean research established that high levels of social contact and cooperation in rural communities often correlated with high levels of conflict (Whyte 1975). In the analytical framework of social capital, intracommunity fights indicate failed understandings, lack of trust, or some other pathology. Yet, in many Andean communities disagreement might not only be a regular part of life, but may perhaps even be a necessary step on the way to promoting local development (Colloredo-Mansfeld 2009). A theory about the social side of economic action must account for disagreements amid collaborations, to recognize that some differences grow from wider connections. It is here that a more precise notion of "public economy" could be an important idea for place-based economies.

To be considered a public economy, production and commerce should have three qualities. First, owners, tradespeople, and workers need to come together as participants in conversations about matters of general interest, not mere private matters (Habermas 1989). Of course, what these matters of general interest are may not be clear until after the conversations. Some interactions begin as private business affairs only to broaden when the goals of the individuals diverge and people reach for new allies in the course of their debates. The public sphere is a field in which "plans and projects emerge that are less a consensus achieved by private persons and more a compromise between conflicting private interests." To further borrow from Habermas, in a public economy, people regularly subject programs "to the public use of reason" and decisions are "susceptible to revision before the tribunal of public opinion" (Habermas 1989, 235).

Second, a public economy establishes itself within a particular type of power relation: it is a restriction on the influence and reach of the state and concentrated private interests, including corporations or a cartel. Writing about computer programmers and the Internet-based community of free software, anthropologist Christopher Kelty (2008) writes that programmers understand the Internet to be a place of work, a technology, a market that represents a moral order. It has to be protected if it is to retain its essential democratic character, and in standing up for an open and shared public technology, creators of free software assert themselves as "a check on other constituted forms of power" (Kelty 2008, 7; see also Coleman 2013). If the artisan trades of provincial Andean towns seem far removed from free software, the preoccupation with the concentration of economic power is not. A public economy creates itself by defending the autonomy of small participants.

Third, a public economic sphere has real material stakes for participants. More than a space of opinion, expression, and politics, that which is public and shared also adds the tangible value that makes business profitable. In an artisan textile town, such values can be in the repeated details of fashion and designs, the reputation for product quality, and visitor traffic. Indeed, when a small business has no practical way to build its own reputation and when it can earn dependably from the town's elevated business activity, the public sphere may act as a kind of essential economic commons. Thus, participants in the public conversations find themselves in relations of mutual economic dependence, tied more acutely to their neighbors than others who live in hidden (or more individualized) local economies.

This is a variant of the theme of invasive trades. It begins with narrow commercial networks, yet emerges over time as a widely defining feature of both economic and civic life such that all events in town must engage with a new signature trade, whether they want to or not. Whereas the previous chapter analyzed how this happens in an open market plaza, Atuntaqui provides an example of an artisan public economy that did not start with marketplace visibility. This artisan public economy becomes possible when business operators claim to work for the general community interest, not just private profit (which once again becomes deeply skewed); when those claims can be openly disputed by others; when people stand up for the autonomy of their trade against corporations and the government; and when the real economic value of one business cannot be broken free of neighboring businesses.

In the following sections, we detail the elements of Atuntaqui's transformation toward a public economy. We begin with the reorganization of workshops around larger cutting tables and the remodeling of stores around new brand names. We then discuss the expansion of a commercial trade show to a civic event, and the reclaiming of both an enormous old factory and a pre-Columbian indigenous site as cultural patrimony. However, we also explain how the public economy is threatened by contracts with chain stores, the booming real estate market, and new government initiatives. Like the cut-throat competition described in the Otavalo market plaza, the economic and cultural initiatives in Atuntaqui were probably never meant to create this public economy. And yet the cumulative consequences of these initiatives brought a fragile public sphere into being. We conclude with observations of what it might take to bring Atuntaqui's public economy back, as well as lessons from Atuntaqui for others attempting to build local public economies.

Before the Fashion Center, Atuntaqui Was a Factory Town

Decades before the government initiatives of the 2000s, family-owned textile businesses expanded and diversified on their own. The Atuntaqui textile industry first took shape in the shadow of the massive Fábrica Textil Imbabura, the Imbabura textile factory, a manufacturing operation set up in in the 1920s with capital from Spanish investors, two brothers named Francisco and Antonio Dalmau (Posso Yépez 2008). At its height, the Imbabura factory employed more than six hundred workers and supplied markets throughout Ecuador and southwestern Colombia (see figure 24). Yet as early as the 1950s, retired workers and other

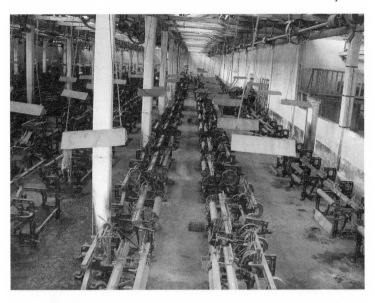

FIGURE 24. The abandoned electric looms, Imbabura textile factory (Photo: Rudi Colloredo-Mansfeld)

entrepreneurs set up alternative home-based weaving businesses. As the Imbabura factory went into decline, first through a lack of investment and then as a consequence of labor strife, family-based artisan operations came to dominate local manufacture, producing acrylic cloth, sweaters for regional markets, and local school uniforms. Then from the 1970s, growing numbers of Atuntaqui artisans moved beyond knitted cloth, diversifying into sporting apparel. For sporting clothes producers, the most significant growth occurred before 2000.

The new operations, however, preserved old business habits, even as their owners lost confidence that those tactics would bring success. In 2005, ex-mayor of Atuntaqui Luis Yépez explained that the artisan trade had been built on "hidden factories." They were hidden in part because of their informality and their artisan, home-based production techniques, but also because sales were realized through closed networks of private resellers. A group of owners worried about the future of this way of working and came to Yépez in 2000 seeking technical and marketing assistance. As Yépez related, "They said to me, 'if we don't change we are going to die.' With the woolen sweaters only one business was going to survive. If there were others they would have to connect to this one. How cruel. Hundreds once made sweaters and now they would be out of work."

Looking back on the changes he encouraged, Yépez insisted that the most important idea was that the business owners should work together: "The whole world is changing. Everyone is associating to strengthen themselves." Such association mattered to develop joint marketing efforts in order to attract new outside interest. It also mattered "to give a start to a change in mentality" in Atuntaqui. Indeed, in the early 2000s, important technical changes were often quite simple individually, but became more complicated as they required changes on the shop floor, among workers, and with suppliers. To sustain the will to press on, through all of these fronts, the cluster consultants encouraged shop owners to give up their customary secrecy, embracing solidarity with other operators who sought change.

To speed up production, for example, shop owners wanted to standardize the sizing, piecing, and cutting of designs. It turned out the complex changes began with replacing perhaps the simplest technology in the shop: the cutting table. Some shops had the industry-standard tables with large smooth surfaces, but most did not. Some relied on sheets of plywood with deep ballpoint pen marks along their edges, little grooves to measure out different sized garments. In an early quality improvement program, consultants urged owners to acquire larger tables and reorganize workspaces around them (see figure 25). Many did, with some of the largest new tables stretching to 27 square meters of surface area.

But to fully take advantage of the new cutting tables, workshops needed to adopt a larger packet of innovations. Employees in charge of preparing the cutting had to anticipate all the needed sizes and make efficient use of fixed patterns to avoid waste from excessive scraps. Owners had to purchase carriages

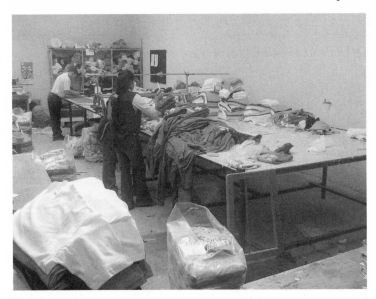

FIGURE 25. Sorting pieces after cutting fabric on large new cutting table (Photo: Rudi Colloredo-Mansfeld)

for rolls of cloth so that one hundred sheets of fabric could be laid out and cut at a single time. New cutting tools had to be purchased. Workers had to learn new skills. Most importantly, realizing real cost savings meant the whole process from design to sizing to planning to cutting needed to be integrated by using computerized plotters.

Studies of innovation have underscored how often big changes require solving a multitude of small ones. A move to a radically new way of performing a task "requires the creation of suitable working parts and supporting technologies" (Arthur 2005, 5). For family businesses and artisans, social institutions and cultural values themselves can be part of the working parts and building blocks of innovation (Winslow 2009). In Atuntaqui, municipal officials and outside consultants made it possible to critically examine and change ingrained habits of artisan production by intentionally remaking social ties in the course of technical training. In giving up the old benefits of secret workshop knowledge, the owners gained new partners who could assist in pulling together all the working parts needed for high-volume production.

Located in backrooms and top floors of Atuntaqui manufacturing facilities, new cutting tables were not public in a strict sense. During the early years of the quality improvement program, workshop visits were limited to a small and homogenous group of men and women. Many of these producers were already linked by kinship. Yet for all those limitations, in the course of setting up their new tables, dedicated apparel makers were breaking old habits of secrecy, interrupting the insulated, idiosyncratic production that can be so typical of artisan manufacture.

As important as these production changes were, the public economy really began when owners rebranded their businesses and promoted their brands through renovated stores. Certainly some businesses had invested in building the reputation of their name and store, with significant remodeling efforts in the 1990s. But from 2000, owners reoriented toward shorter brand names aimed at attracting consumers rather than promoting a family name to intermediaries. From within the town of Atuntaqui, these names—Panda, Conga, Karmam—spread on billboards along the Pan American Highway, in big banners hung over shop windows, and with franchise operations elsewhere in the highlands (see figure 26). Of course, a private brand is not really an emblem of a shared public economy. Each owner embraces a logo to set a single business apart from rivals. However, in Atuntaqui the creation of new brands became intensely interactive—it spread like a contagion, causing building after building to give way to glass-fronted showrooms.

One after the other, businesses moved closer to each other, concentrating in the center of town. When one store moved to a bright modern building, its competitor made a similar move. Others stayed in the same location but changed names. Between 2005 and 2011, clothing stores in the center of Atuntaqui underwent 194 changes—opening new branches, moving, changing names, closing, remodeling (see figures 27a, 27b). Hundreds of private investments in separate branded stores built a new shared

FIGURE 26. Branded billboards along the Pan American Highway (Photo: Rudi Colloredo-Mansfeld

urban space of fashion and apparel. As the spending gathered momentum, the emergent civic sphere of business cooperation physically showed itself as a bright streetscape of shop windows, fashionably clad mannequins, big posters promising sale prices, and overhead signs with trendy names. These were private

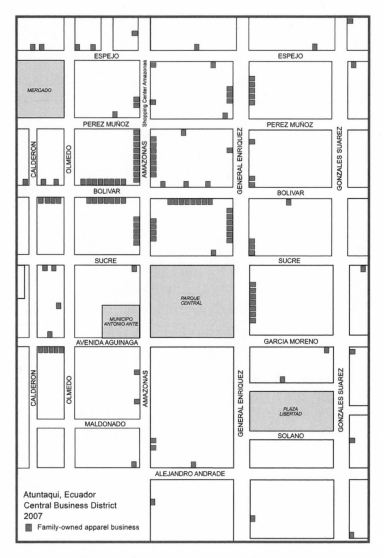

FIGURE 27A. Grouping of apparel retailers in central Atuntaqui, 2007

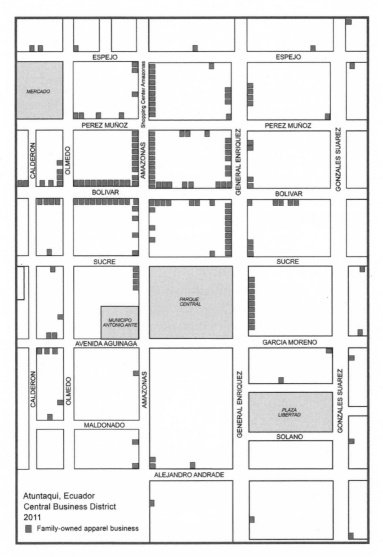

FIGURE 27B. Grouping of apparel retailers in central Atuntaqui, 2011 (Map credit: Brett Riggs, used by permission)

establishments, but the shops had multiplied to jointly claim the urban zone as a fashion showcase. The whole town resembled an upscale market plaza.

True public debate about the meaning of the Atuntaqui transformation began with arguments over Expoferia, the annual marketing event that put Atuntaqui on the map in 2001. Aiming for business beyond short-term sales, organizers used the exhibition to showcase not so much products but the ideal of competitiveness. It was a demonstration not only of individual producers or one industry, but of a dynamic economy—the productivity of the town and region. In 2001, agriculture made a big play for attention. For the first event, the stands of food and farm products outnumbered textile stands, and the agriculturists drew on a longer tradition of agricultural fairs and festival competitions to plan their participation.

Timed to coincide with the Carnival holiday weekend, the first Expoferia drew large crowds. The visitors consumed enthusiastically—primarily casual clothes. In response, the next year the number of apparel makers with stands at Expoferia tripled, from 24 to 72. By 2004 the number of agricultural products stands had fallen from 34 to just 4, and by 2007 the focus of the event had so narrowed to clothing that agricultural stands were no longer counted as a category.

Each year the school grounds that had been used as an exhibition hall became so congested with visitors that the Chamber of Commerce in 2004 began searching for a new tradeshow arena. They briefly considered building a stand-alone hall designed specifically to promote fashion, but then changed course. Rather than isolate tradeshow traffic in a building on the urban margins, they reconceived the show as a street fair, integrating fashion runways, cultural performances, and exhibitors' displays around the main plaza and along the central blocks of the town's main avenues. Working with a Quito-based team of designers and public relations consultants, they developed posters, banners, brochures, and a color scheme for signs, stages, stands, and even bathrooms and light posts. To cover the costs, they continued the custom of charging entrance fees. However, in 2006 they erected a fence around the central blocks of Atuntaqui, concentrated the cultural programming inside the fence, and posted a price of US$1 to enter. For the five days over Carnival, even Atuntaqui residents had to pay to enter their own city. The protests began.

From the organizational phases of Expoferia 2006, provincial newspapers reported citizens' outrage at having their town's streets and plaza privatized by the Chamber of Commerce. Letters to the editor complained of basic violations of citizens' rights and the financial hardship of paying merely to enter their own neighborhood. Others pointed out the basic unfairness for the stores located just outside the fences.

Organizers with the Chamber of Commerce had worried about these issues. They tried to place the fences to be as inclusive as possible and offered to rent stands to businesses on the outside of the trade show district. They also tried to keep the costs low. Their intention had always been to widen the event and make it more accessible, even at the cost of dispersing the revenue that had once been concentrated among the seventy textile stands at previous trade shows. As Angelo Placencia, a producer and officer with the Chamber of Commerce, said in 2006, "even though it actually hurts me, [hosting Expoferia in the city center] is a good thing. We'll leave this selfishness and do something more democratic."

Public opinion, however, was against them. And it was truly public, a debate that took place in the newspapers, spanning several weeks. Ultimately, municipal authorities were persuaded about the unfairness of the entrance tickets and the Chamber of Commerce stopped charging the fees. Having pushed an all-encompassing partnership between textile industry and Atuntaqui, the owners found their position downgraded. They looked to create "something more democratic" and that democracy came to life. Public opinion insisted that the town itself was not merely an instrument for textile sales. Atuntaqui would not be beholden to a single trade, no matter how successful.

At the time of the Expoferia dispute, citizens began asserting themselves in other ways. The fledgling public economy of the early 2000s was followed by two cultural heritage projects, which, although not directly economic, picked up on businesses' new habits of public engagement. The first project involved the recovery of the Imbabura factory and the second was the rehabilitation of Paila Tola, an ancestral pyramid base. The municipal government had successfully worked with citizens and gained national cultural patrimony designations for each, the Imbabura factory in 2001 and Paila Tola in 2004.

Of the two locations, the Imbabura factory inspired the most ambitious plans. Ex-mayor Yépez had been instrumental in securing the cultural designation and promoted the re-use of the huge textile plant as both a museum for the old industry and a meeting ground for the new one. As the coordinating ministry for natural and cultural patrimony promised in a report, a remodeled Imbabura factory "will make a great center for artisan exhibition, tourist information, youth house, and other spaces for the arts" (Ministerio Coordinador de Patrimonio Natural y Cultural 2009, 6). For its part, Paila Tola enjoyed more dynamic civic programming. Beginning in 2003, a formal association of indigenous and mestizo residents made the ancient pyramid the spiritual base of newly revived Inti Raymi celebrations, an Andean solstice festival that was prominent in neighboring Otavalo and had been celebrated in the districts around Atuntaqui.

There was much to connect the cultural projects with the competitiveness and textile cluster programs. In practical terms, the different initiatives shared the same leaders. Elvia Maigua, for example, served as both the treasurer of the Chamber of Commerce and the president of the Corporación Atahualpa, the association that brought the Inti Raymi festivities back to Atuntaqui. Richard Calderon served as first president of the Chamber of Commerce and then went on to be the mayor, where he supported a number of economic showcases at the Imbabura factory. Textile shops have offered either financial backing or their companies' participation in programming related to Paila Tola or the Imbabura factory. As apparel makers sought publicity, managers working with heritage projects were able to provide venues and audiences. Moreover, cultural patrimony worked to attract attention from the growing crowds at the annual textile showcase. The more popular Expoferia became, the more opportunity these heritage sites had to share their significance. In a culmination of these efforts, some of the cultural activities and fashion shows for Expoferia have been held in the renovated spaces of the Imbabura factory.

Interestingly, municipal authorities took advantage of the open participatory planning sessions for the competitiveness projects to garner support for cultural projects. The meetings of the Chamber of Commerce became venues to explain progress on the Imbabura factory project. Municipal authorities, in fact, recruited the two of us as investigators from our project with the Chamber of Commerce, encouraging us to extend our textile research to include an oral history project on the Imbabura factory. In 2006, municipal authorities issued a press release on these oral history interviews and recruited ex-workers through a regional newspaper article about our project in *La Hora*. Municipal authorities then worked with Ibarra-based researcher Miguel Posso on a more comprehensive documentary history of the Imbabura factory and sponsored four open dialogue sessions where ex-workers could come and share their memories for posterity (Posso Yépez 2008). Just as the modernization of clothing production moved from technical improvements for individual workshops to a city-wide enterprise, the preservation of cultural patrimony moved from bureaucratic initiative to wider public interaction. Industry and heritage each learned open habits of self-development as part of an emergent public economy.

The public economy in Atuntaqui could be seen as growing incrementally. A few owners first opened up to ex-mayor Yépez about their problems. Then a larger group opened up their workshops to each other. They and others then opened new stores along Atuntaqui's streets and together they all used a trade show to open their town to the nation for business. These openings did not necessarily build linearly on one another, but rather enabled different types of interaction. The participants in the quality improvement program were largely in the private world of shop owners; their conversations were narrowly interested and trade related. The store construction and remodeling included more and more businesses, but the action was individualized. The project of turning Atuntaqui into an open-air shopping mall by debuting one store after another was an exercise in one-upmanship. It was reactive and particular even as its results were collective. In contrast, Expoferia required direct cooperation. Its spectacular growth subsequently called for planning. And ultimately this talk around the trade show served as a catalyst of public debate about just how important textile production is to Atuntaqui, about the value of its annual trade show, about the preservation and use of its cultural heritage, and about the inclusivity of its development. For all the different interactions, participants worked together to shed old habits of secrecy and create new public currents in the economy and in municipal administration. But for all its success, this public economy has become fragile and threatened.

The Public Economy Slips Back into the Shadows

Several of the threats to Atuntaqui's public economy emerge directly from its successes. The most notable hazard comes from finally achieving both the production capacity and quality controls that enabled producers to sell large quantities to retail chain stores. From the beginning of their quality improvement programs, manufacturers aspired to quality mass production that would meet international standards. The clearest indication that they achieved this capacity came when several of the fast-growing national chains signed contracts to substitute Atuntaqui-made products for imports from Peru, Colombia, and elsewhere. New Ecuadorian government tariff policies gave such sales a big, but temporary, boost.

Workshops began to secure orders for 10,000 to 15,000 units. As they hired workers to meet their obligations, they found that the larger the sale, the harder it was to preserve their financial independence. Other sales to older clients took a backseat to meeting the delivery schedules for the large chains. Their customer base narrowed and large retailers gained even more clout over the Atuntaqui producers. Worse, working for the chains required huge up-front costs in labor and materials. The large corporations' payment schedules of 90 to 120 days meant Atuntaqui manufacturers needed bank loans to cover short-term cash flow. "The chains just play with your money," one owner complained in 2010. In order to cope with debt they had incurred, she said, "We need to shut one of our stores. Shut our pride." Aside from shifting business away from the retail landscape of Atuntaqui, chains also erased business identity by obligating suppliers to mark their products with the chain's own brand names.

One Atuntaqui operator who had the capacity to meet chain-store orders initially refused to take on the work. He saw the chains as a threat. "Recently people have been working with the chains. The chains came here and I said 'no.' Why? Because I have orders, I have work, I have my children, my house. We've been working twenty years. So it could start to scare me. So I didn't do that." Still, the need to secure enough contracts to pay for his machinery and his workers caused him to work more and more as a small sweatshop garment assembler, or *maquiladora*, for Quito firms. In the summer of 2011, he was handling one order for 200,000 T-shirts, work that eliminated the chance of producing any of his own styles for six weeks. With no material costs to worry about, he had little financial risk. At the same time, he felt he had placed the fortunes of his business in another operator's hands.

This has been an irony in the competitiveness training in Atuntaqui: the cluster consultants urged owners to invest in industrial identity to get a piece of the national market, both as individual brands and a citywide reputation for fashion. In fact, bringing a cluster of businesses to national and international standards is part of the script for competitive-advantage success. However, having finally achieved the capacity to do large-scale business, Atuntaqui owners now find that the chains have been dismantling store-brand identities as a condition for getting a share of the chain's business.

Changes within Atuntaqui have also confined a portion of new economic activity to the shadows. Most notably, the boom in real estate in the commercial district led to a hyperactive property trade disconnected from the actual brands on the storefronts. Even as the number of visitors to Expoferia fluctuated from year to year, the number of new stores continued to rise. Much of the new building was concentrated in the blocks that were promoted by Expoferia. In the five years since the relocation of the trade show in 2006, the number of apparel business with a retail presence grew from 110 to 238. And as the density increased, rents likewise rose dramatically for spots with the highest visibility. In some of the newest places, six to eight businesses shared the ground floor, with each paying $600 to $800 monthly for their space. Such earnings sent land prices soaring, with prime downtown commercial lots selling for US$400,000. Of course, real-estate transactions have always been a private, hidden economy. What has changed has been the shifting balance of profitability between landlords and apparel producers. As rents ate up more of the retail economy, the economic players profiting from the textile trade may have had little to do with the clothing designers themselves.

Owners have also retreated from the public sphere in reaction to new government policies, especially stricter labor regulation and enforcement. Such regulatory oversight was overdue. A decade of growth and the sharp rise in volume during the initial wave of chain-store orders put a lot of pressure on workers in the most successful shops. The women operating the sewing machines began to lodge more complaints with labor inspectors. One owner admitted to facing more than thirty formal labor complaints in a two-year period from 2008 to 2010; she needed a year to pay off her fines. She said that her clothing business had been put on an intensive inspection schedule and she had thirty-five visits from government officials in 2010–2011.

She and other apparel producers have responded by dismissing workers and subcontracting work to the growing number of small maquiladora sweatshops within Atuntaqui. One business cut its workforce from 87 employees to just 17, contracting with 7 small producers. The owner noted that a single garment cost him US$1.87 in wages when made in his own shop, but only $0.98 when he subcontracted the work. Even smaller producers have shifted to this model. A business that had once employed eight operators at its largest dropped back to two, subcontracting production to three smaller operations. Yet another operator who was expanding his subcontracting explained: "They can be very productive. All they do is work and eat. They work until 6:00 or 7:00 at night. They are outside the rules of the workshop."

Here again the success of the quality programs that drove the growth of workshops also enabled this subsequent reduction in size. Equipped with computerized design programs, plotters, and large-scale cutting machinery, workshops can efficiently design clothes and prepare material, which can then be assembled elsewhere. Hundreds of ex-workers in the town are trained on the latest industrialized sewing machines, have money from their severance pay to acquire their own machines, and have set up their own businesses to serve as the labor force for the brand-name businesses. Some of these smaller operators are poised to grow and take their place among established businesses; others have joined the Chamber of Commerce and indicate a willingness to join training programs and other projects to collectively build the trade. Many are not only "outside the rules" and outside of public scrutiny, but must remain so if they are to be economically viable.

In a way, this is perhaps the beginning of a new round for the invasive trade. In this new disruption of the barely established model of small, high-quality branded producers, scores of similarly skilled maquiladoras have surged into a new market niche. What once was an invasive trade of small artisan shops in the 1980s was able to routinize, become a public economy, and provide a broader base of benefits in the 2000s. However, this very success—enabling some to exit the artisan sector and develop larger, high-profile operations that had to be governed by labor standards and minimum-wage laws—effectively bid them out of competition. The only way they could survive was to scale down their workforce and contract with cottage industries. This is one of the most troubling things that can happen when "everyone becomes an artisan" (see chapter 1)—a competitive bid-to-the-bottom cycle of home-based self-exploitation.

The cultural patrimony projects also retreated from public view. Having rallied residents to keep the Imbabura factory and Paila Tola from falling to ruins, municipal planners entered a new phase, focusing on state ministries to secure needed funds for renovations. They have succeeded admirably. In 2009, tourism authorities in Atuntaqui took advantage of the national government's "Emergency Cultural Patrimony Decree" and received more than US$1 million for emergency roof repairs on the Imbabura factory. Since then, the Imbabura factory project has received two larger grants: another US$2 million for physical repairs and renovations and a separate US$1.4 million to develop a fashion institute that would be housed in the remodeled sections.

Paila Tola's renovation is already complete. With national funds, the municipality was able to clean up the whole site, fence it in, install a network of paths, and construct a gateway house. They gained security, but at the cost of accessibility. Visitors now need to walk door to door in a nearby neighborhood to find the local guard to get a key to open the gate and enter the Paila Tola. The professionalization of the preservation efforts invites less participation. These cultural monuments are no longer a meeting ground for local engagement.

Spelled out like this, the recent changes in Atuntaqui do not appear to reflect a new stage of competitive development. Rather, old habits of secrecy seem to be choking the potential of the public economy. Private contracts between big operators in Quito and the Atuntaqui producers have left the provincial manufacturers vulnerable. As the economy matures and the local retail market saturates, economic power begins to shift from vendors to landlords. As the state reasserts itself with protections for workers and taxes for social security, operators retreat into informality, back into even more hidden artisan-style workdays and workshops. And as cultural patrimony receives formal state patronage, citizens stand by to let professionals steer the course. In all this, business owners have not so much gone into hiding as gone quiet. The stores still line the streets. A few of the smaller manufacturers are joining the Chamber of Commerce. And yet fewer apparel makers are renting stands at Expoferia or joining debates about where to invest next in the collective promotion of Atuntaqui.

During interviews in 2011, owners talked about the future of their businesses, worried about the labor policy of the government, and explained how they would try to match their labor force to the contracts they thought they could win. This talk of business development, though, had been uncoupled from discussion of Atuntaqui's collective development. The economic value that had spread out across the collectivity, the value that came with being "Made in Atuntaqui" no longer attracted the discussions and investments that it had just five years earlier. There was a new boundary between business and civic life. In 2005, manufacturers spoke as if being a better operator meant both standing together with other operators and building a better town. In 2011, being a better operator meant simply being able to stay in business, out of debt, and in pursuit of steady sales.

Regaining a Public Economy

César Paredes's analysis of the Atuntaqui cluster experiment singled out the problems: exploitation of the labor force, price undercutting, failure to develop complementary industries, and the overall loss of economic diversity. Paredes lays the blame on an initiative that favored a small number of well-connected firms within a single trade. Our research partially affirms his argument. The shift of production to small, economically vulnerable operations of ex-workers, the saturated retail streetscape, and the retreat of agriculture producers from Expoferia indicate structural problems for the town and regional economy. The costs of overspecialization endure.

Nevertheless, such problems do need to be placed in the context of obvious successes. Over a ten-year period, the apparel industry grew, workshops mastered the basic computerized design systems and streamlined production techniques, sewing machine operators found willing employers, provincial manufacturers maintained their market in the face of imports, and the town attracted tens of thousands of visitors. More to the point, the cluster initiative insisted on sharing a commitment, to looking to competitors as allies in solving the practical problems of remaking goods, jobs, and a civic identity. This social approach lifted a wide set of economic and civic initiatives.

As successes grew, the circle of participants widened. The vision for remaking Atuntaqui into a fashion center grew more ambitious. Finally, the apparel producers overreached in the 2006 trade show when they turned the heart of the town into a private Chamber of Commerce convention hall. There were limits to the value and scope of the industrial cluster. This give-and-take over the entrance fees to Expoferia, though, indicated just how public the hidden factories of Atuntaqui had become. Private citizens, Chamber of Commerce leaders, municipal authorities, independent apparel businesses, and other Atuntaqui business owners had to negotiate plans for Expoferia and the place of textiles in general. Narrow interests of the powerful firms within the cluster had to make room for more inclusive options. In 2006, a businessman could reason that even if relocating the trade show into a wide public venue would cost him customers, he could support it because it was more democratic. Firm owners at the time acted as if their business responsibilities were also civic ones.

Just when the cluster developed this civic capacity, the spirit of collaboration weakened. More than that, the shared economics of trade show, "city of fashion" joint marketing, and collective manufacturing improvements started to lose value. Part of the problem lay in the inherent contradictions of modern apparel manufacture. The better a firm became at managing the latest global production techniques, the more it had to compete globally. With more machinery and workers, operations needed to secure larger contracts and compete internationally to boost profits on ever smaller margins. Working the large retail chains turned out to be a cold, hard lesson in the downside of success.

The weakening public economic sphere also had an organizational dimension. Indeed, four steps could have been taken, or could still be pursued, to restore a vital civic current to economic life and broaden employment, tourism, and product innovation. First, the diversity of the economy—the varied agricultural sector, the older tourism around restaurants, local food, and other businesses—could be brought into Chamber of Commerce trade shows and heritage projects. This was a clearly lost opportunity. The original 2001 Expoferia demonstrated the willingness of the agricultural sector to seek a new, shared competitive footing for their business. Incorporating agriculture may have interfered with short-term strategic partnerships among textile operators— the narrow development of one group's social capital. However, it might have built a more resilient civic economic organization in the long run.

Second, municipal officials and the Chamber of Commerce leaders needed to cooperate in 2007 to achieve a new, sustainable revenue stream for the city-center Expoferia. Having insisted on an open street fair, city officials then left the Chamber of Commerce in an untenable position, asking them to deliver all the benefits of the event without a way to pay for it. Ever since, the programming has not been as ambitious as it was in 2006. Worse, the Chamber of Commerce has never again been debt-free. This financial burden scared away potential leaders and members of the chamber.

Third, the Chamber of Commerce and other associations of economic life need to keep up with the recent organizational changes in textile production—the shrinking of large labor forces within established firms and the rapid growth in the number of subcontractors. The ex-workers who now labor in their own homes need their own opportunity to get technical assistance, public exposure, and a say in how to develop the provincial economy. The cluster needs to be reimagined.

Finally, there is a need to incorporate greater public participation in the direction of cultural heritage efforts like the plans for the Imbabura factory and Paila Tola. Our oral history interviews in 2006 demonstrated reluctance among residents to create private museum spaces, but instead spaces that would stimulate what could still be a diverse array of economic participants. As places outside the overbuilt town center, these areas are opportunities to improve the streetscape and conditions for those who have been excluded from the retail and real estate boom.

Atuntaqui has successfully demonstrated how to reinvent a trade and reinvigorate civic spirit in the process. Local residents can remember and recapture those lessons while they are still fresh. Indeed, there may be wider lessons for towns trying to build public artisan economies in the wake of deindustrialization, a topic we revisit in the concluding chapter.

6

Designing Dreams: Innovation and Tradition in the Artisan Cultural Commons

This chapter considers Ecuadorian President Rafael Correa's inaugural shirt and the theme of innovation adopted by countless evangelists for institutional change (or mere job security) around the world. Behind the success of Correa's shirt is a captivating backstory of three women melding into an unlikely collaborative team: a fashion designer, an apparel shop owner, and an embroiderer who all worked feverishly to deliver the final shirt. But despite their success, the collaboration did not endure. In our interviews with these women, we trace different visions of nation, innovation, and tradition, as each finds both success and frustration. We also trace the shirt's journey as it reenters the Otavalo Indian Market as another inexpensive knockoff.

Our aim in this chapter is to replay those moments of collaboration and triumph, recapturing and conveying some of those hopes. We then attempt to faithfully document the discordant aftermath, not as a cynical warning that all hopes must fall apart but more as a chronicle of possibilities. One woman represents a quite clearly articulated vision for economic development that might nevertheless be exclusionary. The others are less thought through as business plans, yet embody practices that might be more broadly supported for a community. At a time when the industrial capitalist version of modernity has faltered, it is important to consider these sometimes jostling possibilities. These are voices and practices that might be lost in the lure of programmatic statements about innovation and artisans issued by elites and government planners.

Latin America's New Leftist Clothing Crisis

In 2006, Rafael Correa confronted a clothing crisis as a newly elected, left-leaning Latin American politician trying to join an emerging club of like-minded presidents. Correa could have drawn from the iconic symbols of the left, the well-worn tradition of Fidel Castro's military uniforms, Mao's suit, or Nehru's jacket. Then there were the Andean leaders whose garments seemed to speak to being "of the people," like Venezuela's Hugo Chávez and his red shirt or Bolivia's Evo Morales and his alpaca wool sweater (Chen 2001; Montaner 2001; Howard 2010). But this was a risky path, potentially linking Correa to worn-out ideas along with worn-out clothes, drawing criticism for emulating others, or losing dignity.

At the other extreme were the business suits favored by Brazil's Lula da Silva or Argentina's Néstor Kirchner. The business suit could reference the older Marxist idea that politics should matter more than clothes; or it could be a disarming gesture, a way to gain acceptance and recognition while pursuing a more radical agenda; or the well-tailored suit could be a nod back to Gorbachev's reforms of the Soviet Union. The risk of the business suit is that the leader fades into looking just like all the rest, easily mistaken for a proponent of corporatized governance and the homogeneity of globalization (Poster 2002).

Finally, especially for a Latin American leader elected in a country with a significant indigenous population, Correa faced the issue of looking authentic, perhaps even acknowledging indigenous heritage (Colloredo-Mansfeld, Mantilla, and Antrosio 2012). One of the "essential accoutrements of invented tradition" in the Americas has been a national clothing style tapping ancient or cultural traditions (Roces and Edwards 2007, 2). But this is risky too—choosing one style might alienate other groups, and what if there is not a clear indigenous clothing tradition to draw upon?

As Rafael Correa assumed the presidency of Ecuador, he joined the already crowded field of Latin America's new leftist leaders. The least well known and least powerful of the bunch, he not only faced down the clothing crisis, but helped produce the most innovative look of them all. His distinctive shirts, beautifully embroidered with pre-Columbian symbols, won him international attention (see figure 28). Correa has presented his shirts as gifts to Hillary Clinton and Bill Clinton, Hugo Chávez, Lula da Silva, and Evo Morales. The shirts debuted at a key ceremony during the transmission of presidential power in the Andean parish of Zumbagua. In immediate terms, the gathering sym-

FIGURE 28. Rafael Correa in his signature embroidered shirt, Fifth Summit of the Americas, April 18, 2009 (Photo: US government)

bolized Correa's intention to bring Ecuador's native peoples into his Citizen Revolution (León 2010).

Yet a curious substitution happened at the events. Although it was called an indigenous ceremony, the media failed to name any indigenous leaders, to describe native acts and artifacts, or to quote any reactions of the Indian onlookers. The idea of indigenous self-representation—the notion that indigenous peoples speak on behalf of themselves and their own customs (Crow 2010)—seemed to have slipped from the agenda. Rather, the epitome of Indian culture that day was taken to be Correa's own shirt. Imbued with mythological signs, the shirt was elevated as evidence of Correa turning away from global fashion and embracing the nation's ancient heritage. And it was the shirt makers, three nonindigenous women from the northern highlands, who emerged with newfound cultural authority. Put another way, in a sartorial sleight of hand, Correa made protest-hardened Indian peasant leaders disappear. In an instant, Ecuadorians now had a fashion designer, an apparel shop owner, and an embroiderer to interpret the country's native legacy and position a new president.

In this chapter we go along with this trick, at least for the moment. In fact, we would argue that these three women have a lot to teach about economics, commerce, and opportunity, as well as citizenship, collective identities, and culture. Our interest grows from the historic fact that since the 1990s, refashioning small industry has become central to government plans in Ecuador and Colombia. Successive governments sought to remake citizens as entrepreneurs, family-run artisan workshops as competitive enterprises, and provincial trades as industrial clusters positioned for international free trade (see chapter 5). As these three women's careers were built during this time of realignment, they provide a benchmark for what different directions labor and ambition could take in the course of Ecuador's Citizen Revolution, Colombia's Third Way, and the many efforts to tout artisan endeavors around the world (see the prologue).

The stories of these three women also speak to the gendered

context of emerging artisan economies. Although gender was never absent, for the most part our stories of peasant farmers (chapter 2), painters and belt weavers (chapter 3), sweater makers (chapter 4), and textile shops (chapter 5) were stories told to us by men. Men were usually the ones narrating the history, meaning, and political significance of artisan work. Artisan crafts, especially clothing workshops, are classic places where domestic life and public commerce mixes, but too often such manufacture hides women's contributions. And when women successfully contend with men for control of workshops, their labor stops being seen as mere "help" and starts counting as real work in actual trades of the national economy (Femenías 2004, 261–62). But in artisan economies, women too are clearly contending for control of their economic destiny. The Ecuadorian president's shirt makers map out three different paths for woman-centered enterprise.

Beyond business and gender issues, these women speak again to the problem broached in chapter 4: the ownership of original work rooted in a shared cultural inheritance. Given the commission they had—to make a beautiful ceremonial shirt—that task would inevitably interweave popular manufacturing traditions with their own artistic visions and cultural knowledge. Indeed, precisely because the garments arose from President Correa's own vision for a distinctive national product, the shirts tapped a shared Ecuadorian reserve of native and craft traditions. When the women first came together as a team, they took from this reserve, and created the original collection of shirts. In launching a follow-up clothing enterprise, however, they divided bitterly on what it meant to continue to use the primordial Ecuadorian imagery that they refashioned. Where the designer asserted her private intellectual property rights as an artist, the apparel shop owner saw shared, public traditions. For her part, the embroiderer claimed historic patrimony of a particular Andean community. As their differences sharpened, leading to a crisis that would dissolve the partnership, the president himself stayed aloof, defending his designs in aristocratic fashion as highly restricted commodities. Meanwhile, Otavalo indigenous artisans, perhaps the most linked to pre-Columbian textile traditions, have busily appropriated the shirt as another cheap knockoff to sell to tourists.

To understand the stakes that went along with cycles of design, development, exchange, competition, and imitation, we revisit the idea of a cultural commons. As mentioned previously, new writings that span law, native studies, anthropology, and history have remade the idea of a commons, broadening it from shared pastures to shared know-how, designs, and the built-up foundations of social life.

In this work, we have turned to the idea of cultural commons to explain the economic stewardship that takes place in textile towns and craft markets. Now we deepen the discussion of a commons from the infrastructure of a new trade to the practical inputs of an individual's business. We have discussed how economic self-interest and competition can create value that is distributed across enterprises, nudging an invasive new trade toward something more like a cultural commons. And once it is routinized, it can become part of a moral duty: people in the next generation receive a trade from their elders and want to pass it to their children. Even here, politics is never absent. A cultural commons involves a political consciousness in which a livelihood is seen as a right—a right that is "asserted as 'ours' rather than mine or thine" (Thompson 1993, 179).

When tracing the origins of their skills and ideas, Correa's shirt makers offer insights into the meaning of "ours" and "our economy" for contemporary artisan economies in the northern Andes. At times in these conversations, "ours" is the exclusive bond between the maker and the president. At other times, the word refers to the intimate community of birth where the speaker learned her trade. And at still other times, the speaker draws in the entire nation, opening the jealous preserve of the local commons to the wider citizenry as part of a larger hope of building a sovereign and inclusive national economy.

Designing Ancestral Roots

You do not understand. Together with the president, I have changed the history of the country. I brought this idea to fruition. I created an identity between the president of the republic and the ancestral roots of the nation.
«ALICIA CISNEROS, *July 2009*»

In late 2006, newly elected Ecuadorian President Rafael Correa began searching for a distinctive Ecuadorian shirt as he prepared for the inauguration ceremonies. Like so many tourists before him, Correa traveled to the indigenous market of Otavalo, hoping for a shirt that would bear the distinctive spirit of his Andean motherland. He found the designs uninspiring and the quality poor, concerns he shared with campaign worker Sandra Meza. Meza told Correa he was wasting his time in Otavalo. Meza ran a small apparel business in the textile town of Atuntaqui, and she told him she knew what it would take to work with Ecuadorian materials to create something distinctive. In the three hectic weeks that followed, the making of the shirt was similar to the making of a film. Meza would serve in the role of the producer, assembling the creative team and keeping the work on track. The fashion designer Alicia Cisneros was the artistic director and it was her vision of pre-Columbian iconography that underlies the beauty of the shirts. The embroiderer Teresa Casa was the skilled technician with the know-how to get designs from paper into cloth. And through it all, Correa was the movie star who brought the whole effort to life.

Cisneros was uniquely qualified to design Correa's shirt. As a fashion designer, she had trained at prestigious design institutes in Quito and had previously devised outfits for national celebrities including Miss Ecuador 2002 (see figure 29). Cisneros was also an expert in Ecuador's pre-Columbian cultures. Cisneros worked as Professor of Ecological and Cultural Tourism at Quito's Universidad Central, leading students on study trips throughout Ecuador and teaching them about the pre-Colombian collections of the premier Ecuadorian Museum at the Central Bank.

FIGURE 29. Alicia Cisneros (Photo credit: Ramiro Loza Cisneros, used by permission)

Sandra Meza had met Cisneros at a design seminar in Ibarra in 2002. The business services unit at the Catholic University-Ibarra had hired Cisneros to teach provincial clothing producers about designs, sizing, production practices, and finishing. "It was a training course for artisans," Cisneros said. Three years later, Meza turned to Cisneros to help make patterns for a sportswear line. When Meza called again in December 2006, Cisneros thought it would be for more work on T-shirts. Instead, Meza asked, "How would you like to work for the president?"

Cisneros got the call on December 23. She completed sketches in four days. "The president wanted something special," she said. Consequently, she drew up a new kind of garment, an austere white jacket. It was cut long, coming down below the waist, buttoned its full length to a high collar, and had no lapels. Cisneros gave two reasons for first working with a jacket. First, she believed it was appropriate for the formality of the inauguration ceremonies, "I was thinking how he would look at the moment of the presentation." Second, the closed jacket on the broad-shouldered president gave her an ample surface for a bold design statement. Inspired by a ceramic figurine from the Jama Coaque culture (100–500 CE), her sketches featured parallel ribbons of interlocking imagery stretching the full length of the coat. "I was always working with this idea, with the most important details coming from ancestral symbols." Cisneros noted that the Jama Coaque used an advanced textile printing technique based on rolling ceramic seals along the cloth. She offered a contemporary interpretation of such a technique, noting that her designs "do not simply represent culture, they are art."

Correa liked the designs, but rejected the jacket. When Cisneros met with him on December 27, he told her, "I do not want a jacket because I do not want to look like Evo Morales." For Correa, Bolivian President Evo Morales had apparently succeeded in establishing iconic clothing of his own, and Correa did not want to risk a jacket-like item that would cast him as a follower for Morales. Correa redirected Cisneros toward shirt designs and emphasized, "I would like a shirt from here, with cloth from here, and buttons from here." The Ecuadorian authenticity of the item would be in its very threads, not just its overt symbols. Correa then said, "I trust you Alicia. You just need to explain to me what the symbols are about," and left her to design them.

Within a week, Cisneros had designed three shirts. Fulfilling the president's wishes, she sourced material from an Ecuadorian manufacturer, although in the end she hedged her bets. To ensure the highest quality she had some shirts made with Spanish cloth as well. During early January, she had to push back against the owners of the shop where the president procured the rest of his shirts. That owner had interfered with Cisneros's work and sought to dissuade the president from abandoning the traditional suit. She confronted him, insisting "my work is work of the highest quality. You stick with your thing and I will stick with mine." Finally, the rival shirt maker condescended to help Cisneros by offering her the president's measurements. "I already have them. I have embraced the president myself," she told him. And in recounting this retort during our interview, Alicia leaned forward stretching out an imagined tape measure in her hands and circled them around, reenacting the intimate hug of a tailor attending her client.

Meanwhile, both Cisneros and Meza searched for an embroiderer skilled enough to manage the intricate designs. Here the fault lines of their relationship revealed themselves. Seeking both quality and discretion, Cisneros turned to a convent in Quito whose nuns were famous for their needlework. The cloistered sisters, though, said it would cost $120 for each shirt, an unaffordable amount. Meza said that she would seek an embroiderer from Zuleta, in her home province of Imbabura. The women of the community had a reputation for high-quality hand embroidery. Cisneros worried about Meza's decision. "Sandra went to Zuleta, but I feared they would copy my designs. This was my first fear," Cisneros reported. However, she had a greater fear of commercial embroiderers who use computerized machines. "I did not want it done by machine. I did not want to let the designs out into the light of day because they were going to copy me."

After Meza recommended the Zuleta embroiderer Teresa Casa, Cisneros invited Casa down for a test of her needlework. She probed Casa, not only about her craft but about her tact and trustworthiness. She explained to Casa that she could not turn around and make the president's shirt for others. In fact, Cisneros explained that she would be "registering the designs as her own intellectual property." Casa left the meeting with the disassembled pieces of the shirt and the designs intended for each part: collar, chest, and cuffs. Over the next ten days she and her daughter completed sections, shipping them via taxi back to Cisneros. Casa in turn sent her son to meet the taxi in the street, retrieve the package, and deliver the embroidered pieces to her in the studio where she assembled the completed shirt.

Finally, just days before the inauguration, the shirts were finished and ready for a fitting. Entering the president-elect's house through the kitchen, Cisneros held the shirts carefully aloft on their hangers and in protective plastic covers. The president saw her approach and said, "*eso me encanta*" (I love that). As he tried them on, the president's wife and her sister, both originally from Belgium, conversed in French, praising the shirt (*c'est très beau*) and debating the rest of his attire (*pas de cravate*), at which point Cisneros showed that she knew a bit of French and spoke up in agreement that the tie should not be worn. Correa had one final design request. He wanted the collar lowered. Cisneros returned to her studio, stripped the collars off and reshaped them. She explained the final collar was a combination of a Mao collar and a rounded military collar, with a relatively wide gap to distinguish it from the priest's collar. In the end, the shirt lost the severity of the original jacket.

Correa realized his desire to have a distinctive shirt "that shines with something of my homeland, something of my country, not a corporate brand." He wore the shirt featuring the Jama Coaque serpent imagery to the Zumbagua ceremony, and to the next day's events at the Equator, the *Mitad del Mundo* monument, he put on a second shirt of embroidered diamonds featuring spears and shields, symbolizing his militant defense of Ecuadorian sovereignty. Within hours of the president's appearances, the press went to work tracking down the shirt's creator. In response, Cisneros, Meza, and Casa began to relay the meaning, work, and hope that lay behind the shirt.

The intensity of their collaboration did not endure. Cisneros claimed a special relationship to the designs that rested in part on personal identification with them and in part on the reasoning of an artist in an age of intellectual property rights. Cisneros still considers her long-term study of pre-Columbian designs as an integral part of her designing. Indeed, part of what she says makes the designs hers is that "I make what I can and I can explain my designs." Being able to tell their story, to narrate a connection between the current article and the past is part of her proprietary role—as if she were a shaman, interpreting signs, using the artifact to guide the wearer to the design's ancient knowledge. Her ownership is akin to stewardship; she is but a guardian of symbols she holds in trust from those that came before (Verdery and Humphrey 2004). Such stewardship, though, is abstracted from a living community of producers and is instead tied to the professionally trained academics who produce knowledge of the ancient past. Her commons is a rarified one that stands apart from the marketplace.

Working with the president was also deeply personal. She measured him, embraced him, visited with the family in the kitchen, listened to his spouse and her sister chat in their mother tongue, and made clothes for his children. Not surprisingly, when Meza asked Cisneros for a copy of the design for her business, Cisneros denied the request. Meza protested that it was a team effort, and Cisneros said, "You do not understand. Together with the president, I have changed the history of the country. I brought this idea to fruition. I created an identity between the president of the republic and the ancestral roots of the nation."

Yet for all the personal meaning it had for her, Cisneros distilled this project to its purest commercial form. A skilled entrepreneur, she followed a strategy promoted at Ecuador's Ministry of Foreign Trade, Industrialization, Fisheries and Competitiveness in the decade before Correa came to power (Colloredo-Mansfeld and Antrosio 2009). She created commercial opportunity through innovation, captured its value with intellectual property laws, and sought to profit through branded production under the Etnica label that she had trademarked. From the beginning, she saw others, from her collaborators to the president's primary shirt maker, as potential rivals. Cisneros explained that in apparel production "the competition is strong." Meza's request for the designs confirmed her suspicions. Likewise, Casa no longer receives work from Cisneros: "Sadly, they copied, even though I asked that they keep from copying. I have not continued working with her."

At one point, Cisneros tried to match private and social entrepreneurship. An embroidery cooperative from Imbabura wrote to ask if she would like to collaborate. She was open to the idea, she said, because she was the head of her household, a mother raising three boys on her own. In view of her own struggles, she was looking for a way to convert embroidery into "a source of income for older women, handicapped women, single mothers, and other vulnerable women." So, she met with the cooperative leaders, signed a contract that specified the earnings, and stipulated that the women were not to copy her designs. "But it did not end well," she told us. The problem was not imitations, but poor quality. "A piece of embroidery is like a piece of handwriting," she observed. When the women brought together the components of a single shirt, the collars, chest, and cuffs were all mismatched, showing clearly the multiple authors involved. Sometimes the work was poor, and other times dirty. "I ended up throwing most of it away." Cisneros terminated the contract: "People need to join together—but with clear ideas."

Correa won his 2006 election promising to fight Ecuador's economic elite (Bonilla and Montúfar 2008). When inaugurated, he declared that his presidency meant an end to the "night of neoliberalism" when globalization threatened to "turn countries into markets, not nations" (Kintto 2007). The threats were certainly real. From land development laws that pushed to privatize communal landholdings, to the dollarization and the destruction of Ecuador's currency, to the negotiation of free trade with the United States, successive governments seemed to have turned Ecuadorian working lives over to the power of global markets. Yet neoliberalism did not just bear down from the outside. Ecuadorians stepped up to live in the possibilities it offered. If these were not terms many would have chosen, small business owners still sought to make their own history by them. Alicia Cisneros counts among a generation of Ecuadorians who built careers from institutions and ideals that neoliberalism encouraged, from intellectual property laws to a drive to be personally competitive. The branded exclusiveness of her business plans illustrates one way that neoliberalism endures in the new day of Correa's rule. Interestingly, it is the apparel manufacturer, Sandra Meza, who offers a contrasting vision.

Dreaming a National Brand

Business Objective: To raise awareness of working in a team and not leave things in the hands of a single person, this business will empower cooperative work which envelops a single brand called País.

«*Sandra Meza's business plan for Marca País*»

Originally from Cotacachi, a small town known for leatherworking and close to both Otavalo and Atuntaqui, Sandra Meza made her career as an apparel producer and trade leader in Atuntaqui's textile boom (see figure 30). In the early 2000s, Meza ran her own small company making sportswear and fleece pajamas. Along the way, she got into politics, working on Correa's campaign and in community development programs. Riding the publicity of the president's shirt, she worked with a partner to relaunch her business as Marca País, specializing in embroidered shirts. When she and her partner failed to raise enough capital for their venture, Meza took a job as the director of Atuntaqui's union of tailors and fashion designers. As a businesswoman, she

FIGURE 30. Sandra Meza (Photo credit: Sandra Meza, used by permission)

enrolled in design seminars and competitiveness initiatives, yet maintained something of the subversive about her. Meza reinterpreted messages of strategic cooperation for competitive advantage as a call for social solidarity. Her work for Correa reinforced her civic consciousness; her dream of running Marca País would have linked people and profits.

When Meza described her conversations with Correa about the shirt, she indicated the problem was in Otavalo. The town promotes itself as the largest artisan economy in South America. Indigenous manufacturers and vendors have embraced mechanization and their own version of globalization involving networks of intermediaries living around the world (see chapter 4; Lalander 2009; Sarabino Muenela 2007). In Otavalo's success, however, Meza and others feel the products on offer have lost the clarity of a local, Ecuadorian identity. Meza observed that the craft market attracts those seeking authentic Andean culture, but delivers "Peruvian designs, Aztecs, the art of American Indians, but nothing of ours." She said she had to push Correa to think more broadly: "He wanted a condor or something with mountains, but I said, 'no, we have our own pre-Columbian culture. We have art and we need to look there for it.'" When Correa agreed, she then put in motion the effort that led to Alicia Cisneros and Teresa Casa. After Cisneros's repudiation of her business idea, Meza still forged ahead on the wave of publicity the shirt garnered, developing her own versions of the shirt and employing Casa to embroider them. She adopted Correa's phrase Marca País to name her new business and sought to make it a source for the national good.

Her business plan rejected the decentralization and regionalism that figured in the development schemes of both neoliberal governments and indigenous politics, and instead listed the following objective on her 2007 PowerPoint presentation that she prepared for an exhibition of textile entrepreneurs in Quito during Correa's first year in office: "To raise awareness of working in a team and not leave things in the hands of a single person, this business will empower cooperative work which envelops a

single brand called País [país means "country," but was also Correa's political movement], independent of the region where one
was born or lives." Meza's presentation continued: "No single
ethnic group or race or faith or gender or generation will distinguish our products, but rather we offer a grand acceptance to
all strata and all people who know our product. The new trends
among consumers are to prefer more and more our COUNTRY
BRAND." This new national spirit would reach every input—
the cotton cloth woven in an Ecuadorian factory, the tagua buttons harvested in Equatorial lowland forests, the packaging made
from reeds harvested in Andean lakes, and the strings spun from
fibers of the *cabuya* plant. And all of this transformed by laborers
drawn from vulnerable communities and paid a just wage. Meza
saw all of Ecuador as a shared resource, as the commons upon
which she would draw and develop for others.

It would be easy to let Meza's idealism show up Cisneros as
crassly commercial, but that would underplay Cisneros's own pa-
triotism. Indeed, the competing enterprises, Meza's Marca País
and Cisneros's Etnica, represent parallel and linked nationalisms.
For Meza, national belonging means a collective seizing of the
moment—a unified, multicultural nation rising to build a sovereign economy in a globalized era. For Cisneros, nationalism
leads one back to one's core. It means reaching to the deepest
traditions and embracing the nation's true and millennial spirit.
In his 1973 essay, "After the Revolution: The Fate of Nationalism
in the New States," Clifford Geertz labeled the first sentiment
embodied by Meza as "epochalism" or "The Spirit of the Age"
(241). He called the second "essentialism" or "The Indigenous
Way of Life" (241–42).

Their different perspectives can be read in their orientations
toward intellectual property. For Cisneros, the ancestral culture
she recovers is the essence of the shirt, and should be protected
as bounded property. For Meza, the designs are public and mo-
bile. She does not fear copies; copying is the point. In May of
2007, just a few months after Correa had introduced his shirt to
the world, indigenous producers in Otavalo developed inexpensive shirts that used elements of the original design. When we

showed pictures of these knockoffs to Meza, she asked "When were these taken?" "A week ago," we replied. "This has something of our design," she noted. "Now they do have some of our influence. How incredible, no? Now they are making it with identity, before it was only Aztecs." Nor did Meza begrudge the embroiderer Teresa Casa for selling shirts in direct competition with her. "It was never an exclusive contract. I do not see it as a problem that she is making and selling her own products." At some level, Meza's openness is a commercial tactic, positioning herself against Cisneros's exclusive and trademarked designs. Yet it also fits with her professional experience in Atuntaqui where no one ever completely controls a design. The tussle of contemporary apparel production, joint marketing, trade solidarity, and broad civic partnerships rescued Atuntaqui's textile sector from the doldrums. The cultural commons of Atuntaqui requires connectivity and a public economy to regenerate its creativity.

Throughout the late 1990s and 2000s, Meza had tried to become a more competitive businesswoman. As a dutiful entrepreneur in the textile cluster of Atuntaqui, she implemented a variety of improvement initiatives. She also saw limitations to the cluster approach. She observed how an obsession with making the textile sector competitive caused state officials to neglect the once important farming sector. She saw within the textile sector how a dozen of the biggest firms grew much faster than the hundreds of smaller ones. Working on Correa's campaign fueled her aspirations for an inclusive economy, the public economy ideal that had been tentatively possible in Atuntaqui. Launching Marca País allowed her to bring that vision to others.

Marca País failed. Meza lacked the capital to move beyond small batch, artisan production. Despite being connected to the president himself, she never secured credits from officials at the development bank. In the end, the third collaborator in the project, Teresa Casa, charted a more durable, albeit modest, course to success. Ironically, she rated President Correa's contributions to the shirt a distant second to Galo Plaza, president of Ecuador from 1948 to 1952, who died decades before the garment was created.

Honoring Community Crafts

The shirt represented the years of work and the quality of Zuleta. The honor is all Zuleta; the craft is of the women of Zuleta.
«TERESA CASA, *2009*»

"The shirt is the result of a trajectory," Teresa Casa said (see figure 31). When she traces that trajectory, she starts with the Jesuits who once possessed the Zuleta hacienda; recalls Abilina Lasso, the Catalonian owner who introduced embroidery to her upperclass social circle; praises the schoolteacher who democratized the Catalonian embroidery; and credits former President Galo Plaza with initiating the cooperative that opened up the modern embroidery trade (Prieto 2011). Casa does recognize Correa's contribution—"the idea was born with him"—but she does not elevate it. Correa has strengthened Zuleta embroidery, but then, too, it has strengthened Correa. For Casa, the women from her community worked far harder than the current president to establish Zuleta as the homeland for this art.

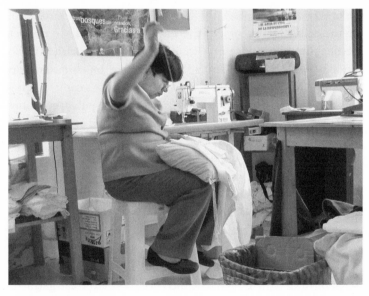

FIGURE 31. Teresa Caza (Photo credit: Juan Carlos Pozo, used by permission)

The mentor Casa venerates above all others was a long-time teacher at the Zuleta primary school named Adela Carascol. Carascol developed classes in drawing and embroidery and organized an annual exhibition to promote her pupils and their work. The exhibition caught President Plaza's eye and he worked with Carascol to establish an embroidery cooperative as a business connected to the hacienda. Casa's own family, though, worked apart. Her mother set up her shop, Cosas Lindas, on the main road outside of the hacienda. Casa and two of her sisters continue to produce for the store. She emphasizes that it has long been, above all else, women's work. "Because we are mothers and wives we had to adapt our work to our responsibilities. There was no time during the day. This was night work." To this day, the embroidery has allowed Casa two main things. The first is that "this work has strengthened the family. It integrates the whole family. It is like a school of life in which the children assimilate the values of responsibility, hard work and being conscientious." Second, it offers an important income: "my livelihood depends 100 percent on embroidered goods."

In the way Casa tells the story, only by knowing Zuleta can you know her personal contributions to the shirt. "The shirt represented the years of work and the quality of Zuleta. The honor is all Zuleta; the craft is of the women of Zuleta. Our community is known at an international level." She came away from the project with gratitude to Cisneros for teaching her about the Jama Coaque. "We did not know that our culture was that rich. I had to study how much added value there was, such a deep meaning, all those symbols, those elements." However, she did not fully share Cisneros's ideas about authorship and control. Rather, her respect for the community inclines her to be accepting of those who copy her. She describes it as a form of aid. "It is a support. My designs can be seen everywhere, computerized and handmade. For me it is gratifying. I take it as a kind of support that I offer others."

Casa sees her productivity as an extension of her community's traditions and in turn reconciles the spread of her profitable designs as a moment of regeneration of their shared work. She is conflicted on this point, though. She works with her husband, Ibarra artist Wilson Sanchez to create new designs. Preserving the sequences of borders from the original shirt, Casa and Wilson have replaced Jama Coaque icons with other pre-Columbian elements. She has also shifted the color palette to earth tones of terracotta, browns, and black. Having described the distortions of her own work in the marketplace, she lamented, "Personally, I wish my designs were registered." She then quickly adds, "but these drawings are the property of all Ecuadorians."

Casa has stitched one set of designs that she neither sells at her shop nor publicizes to the community. These are the shirts Correa continues to order. In a worn manila file, she has archived not only the original inaugural designs, but also newer models created either by Meza or Casa herself. On each sheet, she jotted down the intended bearer of the design, Chávez or Evo; Lula or Alan Garcia; Hillary or Bill Clinton. Some designs have one name, others four or five, including at times individuals from Correa's family. With detailed drawings of mythic serpents, trickster monkeys, shields, spears, and sun gods, all annotated with the heads of state and favored relatives, the protected file contains a complex iconography of presidential power. This exclusive collection reveals, in fact, one of the most authentically pre-Columbian qualities of Correa's shirts. The president echoes the Inca practice of building power through bestowing costly textiles on rivals and allies.

Presidential Stewardship and Prize Shirts

The [Inca] king had certain fabrics reserved for his use alone and his shirts are reported to have been very delicate, embroidered with gold and silver.
«JOHN MURRA, *1962*»

The inaugural shirt risked Correa's public persona on an artisan good with doubtful cultural capital. After all, who wears embroidered shirts with narrow, stand-up, open-throated collars? Tourists? Students during school celebrations of Inti Raymi?

As commentator Carlos de la Torre joked in the Ecuadorian newspaper *Hoy*, if you put on such a shirt, you risk being taken for a waiter at a hacienda-themed restaurant (March 31, 2007). Yet the shirt soon gained political gravitas and prestige. The clarity and beauty of the shirt's designs helped. So too did the explanations of the shirt's symbolism and craft offered by the three women who engineered it. Clearly, though, Correa's own attention to the shirt has made a difference. His innovation was to rescue his shirt from the cheapening cycles of fashion and pop culture. In Bolivia, Morales's casual sweaters and Andean-themed jackets drew from popular styles and inspired further sweaters and jackets based on his own. Morales helped create "a popular and accessible political image" (Salazar-Sutil 2009, 64). Correa, on the other hand, stopped the trickle-down logic of fashion. By denying the shirt to lesser members of his administration, bounding its circulation, and gifting it to the powerful, Correa cultivated a resource for consolidating the presidential image. Correa's politically astute maneuvers recall the tactics of the Inca.

In Andean political history, textiles materialized wealth and power. Skilled rulers used cloth to manage allies and enemies alike. The Inca excelled in this effort. As famed Inca historian John Murra writes, "the king had certain fabrics reserved for his use alone and his shirts are reported to have been very delicate, embroidered with gold and silver" (1962, 719). Having established intimate linkages between his person and types of cloth and clothes, the Inca king subordinated rivals through gifts and prohibitions on use. "The simple fact that a fine cloth . . . had come to be defined as a royal privilege meant that grants of it were highly valued by the recipient, to the point that unauthorized wear of vicuña cloth is reported to have been a capital offense" (Murra 1962, 720). While directing rich textiles to valued subjects, the Inca redefined the identity of the makers so that "the symbolic significance of cloth accrued to the state, rather than to producers" (Costin 1998, 123). Centuries later, Correa grasped the logic. For the president, the shirts became a way to expand his identity and personhood. Clothing others as he is clothed, he magnifies his power.

Even by Inca standards, though, Correa's circle is remarkably restricted. The true Correa shirt rarely appears on anyone else. Indeed, of all leftist presidential fashion—Chávez's red shirt, Castro's hat, and Evo's jacket—none has been so circumscribed as Correa's embroidered shirt. Correa's shirt is, of course, the most tailored, artfully constructed, and expensive. It also has the least precedent in everyday Ecuadorian fashion. It was born apart from the common wardrobe and it has always stayed out of reach. Only in the market plaza Correa rejected—Otavalo's Plaza de Ponchos—are there affordable simple cotton shirts with a stand-up collar and expansive "presidential" embroidery.

Back to Otavalo

Four dollars. In May 2007, indigenous shirt manufacturers in Otavalo paid embroiderers around $4 for the extensive designs that replicated elements of Correa's own shirts. The merchants called the designs "presidential" and sold the finished garments wholesale for around $6. Of course, this was a lot more than the standard embroidered designs, which had been at most $1 per shirt. The newly minted "presidential" embroidery took four times the labor and four times the material as a simple design. Consequently, it cost four times as much. It took four months for the icon of the president, the mythic pre-Columbian roots of the nation, and the national brand to be reduced to their simplest commodity form in the Plaza de Ponchos (see figure 32).

These Otavalo market products represented exactly what Alicia Cisneros feared when artisans got involved in the project. Pirated versions had mushroomed in an uncontrolled street trade; price competition was fierce. For Sandra Meza, too, the Otavalo market and artisan knockoffs corrupted her dream of a new kind of commerce. Wages measured in pennies lock in the poverty of economically vulnerable embroiderers. And in the market stands of Otavalo, Teresa Casa had myriad examples of distorted, care-

FIGURE 32. Otavalo street musicians (Photo credit: Scott A. Diekema, used by permission)

less work. The skill of Zuleta women was hard to find and would go unrewarded in the bulk sales of the plaza merchants.

Yet for all that, the shirt had returned to its legitimate home. Correa himself facilitated this repatriation. Whether intentional or not, with each revision he requested in Cisneros's design, he brought the style of his shirt in line with those of the Plaza de Ponchos. If Meza led Correa away from the market, his own taste returned him to it. Moreover, in the hands of Otavalo's merchant artisans, the president's shirt now had a chance to reinforce a northern Andean provincial economy. The flaws of this market—the copying, competition, cheap prices, poor quality— were also a sign of its democracy. Amidst the woes of sweater makers and others hit by the 2000 dollarization and cheap imports, the cotton-shirt trade was a rare growth industry (see chapter 4). Shirt makers had developed new styles, mixed computerized embroidery and hand embroidery, and found new clients. A few shops had grown quite large, with the largest employing up to fifty seamstresses. Many had already been contracting with women in the Zuleta region long before the Cisneros-Meza-Casa partnership.

In Otavalo, it was not about intellectual property or national identity, but earning profits and making the most of the family business. For these purposes, Correa's shirts offered publicity and trendiness. They were a design resource to be folded into layers upon layers of previous styles from local master weavers, Peace Corps volunteers, Bolivian artisans, hippie entrepreneurs, English knitters, Japanese importers, and international textile consultants. Correa, too, now had found his place in their cultural commons. As vendors in the plaza would say, Correa offered his own "grain of sand" so that the market could "give the daily bread" to working families. An invasive design for an invasive trade now joined the historically invaded community as another resource.

Shirts and Artisan Hopes

What is this new presidential, national-brand shirt made of? South American cotton (on a good day), French embroidery thread, and Ecuadorian Tagua nut; political ambition, creative intuition, and old-fashioned nationalism; artisan knowledge, community traditions, and the skills of apparel technicians; monkeys, snakes, and suns; diamonds, spears, and shields; three women's hopes and one man's dream.

In devising this shirt, Correa wanted to turn away from global consumer brands and express a sovereign, national economy. It was a symbolic gesture to reassert the nation. There is something of an old-fashioned modernism to this nationalism, harkening back to the postrevolution enthusiasm of twentieth-century independence movements. The making of the shirt was meant to rise above internal differences of region, race, ethnic group, and generation. The shirt balanced the tensions Geertz discusses: it expressed a core national essence while capturing something of the spirit of the times.

Consequently, despite all the native symbols, this is not an intercultural garment. The composite nationalism of the indigenous movement, the willingness to let parallel histories, language, laws, and customs develop side by side and in dialog with each other and within a national territory, has gone out of fashion (Whitten 2004).With Correa, a uniform, transcendent nationalism retakes the stage. It rests on a single deep and shared ancestry that can be recovered and articulated by anyone who cares enough to walk in and learn something at an archaeological museum.

The shirt's claim to national authenticity can rest in part on the way Cisneros, Meza, and Casa exploit a distinctly Andean reserve of imagery, institutions, styles, and crafts to create it. We argue that this stockpile of ideas and skills can be thought of as a linked set of cultural commons. They are a commons because they are shared, open and available to the women because of their education, jobs, and interests. They also are a commons because they are democratic, contested, and a platform for challenging elite authority. Finally, this shared economic base is a commons because it requires individuals, at some point, to balance their exploitation of it with the need to preserve, enhance, and pass it down. Casa acknowledges as much when she simultaneously laments the loss of her designs and claims credit for supporting other embroiderers through the infusion of her designs into their repertoire. These elements of the shirt's cultural commons—the sharing, the using, and the regenerating—continue to take a most intense form in Otavalo's Plaza de Ponchos.

The shirt is a result of an invasive trade—mechanized, inexpensive artisan manufacture for bulk sales—that has routinized as a commons. It also brought our own comparative research on Otavalo and Atuntaqui together in unexpected ways, joining the cotton-shirt trade in the Plaza de Ponchos with the public economy that had developed in Atuntaqui, uniting the threads of indigenous commerce with new national symbols.

The cultural commons that make producers fruitful in their work are rooted in a kind of diversity that is often ignored by governments and consultants, even as they busily promote innovation. And it is here that we stop going along with the trick of that inauguration day when Correa stepped in with his handsome, symbol-laden shirt to represent indigenous people, artisans, and peasants. Artisans have worked for decades to represent themselves. In doing so, they have sought to defend the economies rooted in the land and the knowledge of their communities. That is, they have actively defended their commons from elites who sought to enclose their shared pastures, control their water, and devalue their traditions of production.

Peasants in Túquerres, Tigua painters, belt weavers of Ariasucu, vendors in the Otavalo Plaza de Ponchos, Atuntaqui apparel firms, Zuleta shirt embroiderers. Although fraught with tension and inequality, these are places where invasive trades have become routinized as artisan traditions, meshing with older commons and creating new ones. The possibilities are too often fleeting and fragile, but these different, place-based resources sustain vital economic assets. As E. P. Thompson (1993) argued for the English commons, these regional economic bases nurture a political consciousness. This political consciousness measures the progress and shortcomings of government elites, development plans, and the global economy. It speaks to an as yet unrealized vision of a vibrant and just economy that preserves place, identity, and the chance for rewarding work.

Conclusion

Andean Lessons in Artisan-Led Revitalization

In the 1980s, some sharp theorists saw how capitalist mass production was unraveling and that in this time of uncertainty artisan production would find new possibilities. Scott Lash's and John Urry's *The End of Organized Capitalism* (1987), David Harvey's *The Condition of Postmodernity* (1989), and Michael Piore's and Charles Sabel's *The Second Industrial Divide: Possibilities for Prosperity* (1984) looked amid the blight of deindustrialization and predicted the end of national economies in which a few central industries defined social relations and politics (Lash and Urry 1987, 5). Big factories with specialized machinery, powerful labor unions, and national markets dominated by national corporations had been breaking down. More than the ups and downs of regular business cycles, novel forces of cultural and economic fragmentation were at work. Intimate new relations between the developed and developing worlds, the cultural politics of postmodernism, and financial strategies of flexible accumulation have multiplied and subdivided spaces for economic action.

For some writers, decentralized, small-scale production was a foil to a Fordist regime typified by large factories and industrial capitalism. They projected artisan production as little more than the negation of the stability, size, and organization of factory and industrial production. "Self-employed," "consultants, artisans and informal sector," "individualist, anti-monopoly or state regulation," "small family firms (sweatshops)," and "kitchen politics" counted among the qualities of these producers (Harvey 1989, 154). For others, though, the return of small-scale production was innovative. It reopened a pathway to growth that special purpose, mass-production technologies in the United Kingdom and United States had blocked. Piore and Sabel wrote, "these less rigid manufacturing technologies were craft systems. . . . Skilled workers used general purpose machinery to turn out a wide and constantly changing assortment of goods for large but constantly shifting markets" (1984, 5). In advanced economies, a policy for relaunching growth might veer sharply from mass production and "back to these craft methods" (ibid.).

The speculation and theorizing of the 1980s can now be assessed by current ethnographic realities. Or put another way, this book brings back the news of how this fragmented artisan future has turned out so far. We offer what we see as the crucial lessons of craft production and especially the characteristic two-phase mode of artisan-led economic development: first phase, the rapid, invasive spread of novel trades; and second phase, the lively evolution of these trades, which injects a distinctive economic value into public life.

We have offered an original take on both phases. We define the terms of these invasive moments, explaining how risk taking, speculation, winner-take-all competition, and imitation drive this dynamic onward. We have also charted the politics and culture of the new public economic spheres that have arisen: the convergence of identity and commodity design, rise of an ethos of the commons within a marketplace, and the insertion of civic values into the terms of business debates. When some analysts in the 1980s insightfully saw a future in which artisans would return, they offered little direction on how such artisans would shape society. After years spent researching and writing about those artisan worlds, we can present the intensely competitive and deeply interdependent communities that artisans have developed—and the lessons they hold for civically accountable, place-based economies.

On the surface, the Andean producers described in this book can be hard to figure. Assembling new markets with a tweak of an old product, they spark growth that is at times dizzying. Quirky trades penetrate entire towns and remote villages scatter their entrepreneurs across the map. Men who identify as artisans design on laptops, contract with peasant women for skilled needlework, and sell in windy market stalls under the intense mountain sun. A bit like Silicon Valley, profits in Andean valleys are concentrated in the hands of a few through the workings of networks and positional competition. Unlike Silicon Valley, financial hedging can still mean buying and fattening a hog. One year, scores of families are taking big loans and buying machinery. A few years later the equipment is idle, the workshops converted to retail outlets, and the trade show has morphed into a cultural festival.

The jumpiness of artisan trades is not hard to find elsewhere in Latin America. Take, for example, Mexican wood carvers (Chibnik 2003). In the 1960s, the small peasant community of Arrazola in Mexico's Oaxaca valley was just getting by. Many of the households raised corn, beans, and some other staple crops on small subsistence plots. Their land was meager, the soils poor. Some scavenged nearby ruins for small objects that could be sold to folk art dealers. Then an Arrazola resident named Manuel Jiménez partnered with the owners of an Oaxacan craft store to provide wood carvings. The sales grew. Other shops sought out wood carvers to supply them. The craft gradually spread, and by 1985 "there were perhaps ten artisans in the state of Oaxaca who supported their families primarily from the sale of painted wood carvings" (Chibnik 2003, 35). Fifteen years later, about three hundred wood-carving workshops were in operation. Long famous for its weaving, Oaxaca was flooded with brightly painted carvings of animals, human figures, and fantastical creatures. They crowded shelves in craft stores, anchored displays in hotel windows, and perched close at hand in cafés and restaurants. Back in Arrazola, tour buses arrived; cement block houses went up in place of humble huts.

A similar situation arose with Peruvian pottery (Chan 2011). Located in Peru's far north, Chulucanas residents once matched their neighbors in mixing small fruit plantations, artisanal pottery, and basic services. Then, beginning in the 1960s, an innovative spirit grabbed several young men who had grown up among utilitarian potters, fathers and uncles who made great, unadorned ceramic storage vessels for grain and *chicha* (corn beer). The younger men pictured smaller, elegant decorative items. They experimented with the ceramic finishes, smoking the surfaces repeatedly with mango leaves to create dark, earthy reddish-brown and black tones. They researched pre-Columbian imagery for inspiration and looked abroad for customers. A Catholic nun from the United States began to work with the potters, selling to collectors in Peru and around the world. By the 1980s, Chulucanas was home to more than five hundred ceramic producers and the Peruvian national government conferred on the potters the first legally protected denomination of origin trademark for their distinctive style of pottery.

Other less glamorous businesses with artisan roots have also developed. Many of these are in mundane working-class neighborhoods in parts of Latin American cities where tourists rarely venture. The district of Gamarra in Lima, for example, has been a place of manufacture since the nineteenth century, with local families making cloth, working metal, fixing cars, and building furniture. In the early 1970s, residents still felt the district offered a quiet life. Then, within two decades, Gamarra had become the "Peruvian Taiwan." Apparel operations had concentrated within its sixty blocks and a 1993 census recorded "fifty medium sized firms, 1,950 micro and small firms, and 4,100 trading firms selling inputs and final products"; a place that had reached "a boiling point in Peruvian textiles and clothing" (Visser 1995, 7).

Similarly, Tiguan painters can trace their profession to a single, visionary artist. Julio Toaquiza won the patronage of an entrepreneurial gallery in the 1970s. Then other painters taught family members, and neighbors watched (or spied) and tried their hand at painting. Along the way the craft became standardized, and within a decade migrants had sales posts in a Quito park and international clients who would seek them out in the working-class neighborhoods of south Quito. The founding Toaquiza family cast off the commercial dominance of the Quito gallery owners. Leveraging international patronage, they innovated. They painted on ever larger canvases or rendered the brutality of hacienda work in painful detail or layered canvases with symbols of shamanic ritual. By the mid-1990s, Julio's son was jetting abroad. Ten different artist associations advocated on behalf of hundreds of artists living throughout a rural valley and urban working-class neighborhoods in two provinces.

In Otavalo, artisans discussed ways to trademark their own well-known crafts, such as the wedding shirt. Yet most recognized that the market changed too quickly and the habits of copying ran too deep for any kind of intellectual copyright protection. Outsiders appropriated versions of Otavaleño crafts to make distinctive new products. The foreign versions became the platform for designs at the Plaza de Ponchos in Otavalo. Indeed, by the late 1990s, shirt makers poached design details from all sorts of products and producers—hammock makers' fabrics, Zuleta women's embroidery, and their mothers' own sequined shirts. Their products inspired the president of Ecuador as he sought a truly Ecuadorian shirt.

Atuntaqui may not be the "Ecuadorian Taiwan," but we witnessed a proprietor, who was leading us through the workshop behind his house, answer a question about his productivity by taking out a piece of paper with a table on the productivity of Asian factories and explaining how many seconds behind his machine operators were. That moment in 2005 was decades in the making. The huge Imbabura textile factory that began production in the 1920s transformed a place that had been a mule-driver way station into a modern factory town. After the factory's decline, residents built up their own operations in the 1970s and

1980s. When they began to lose customers, they invited consultants to help them innovate. The government-backed quality improvement program pushed individual producers to give up their artisan ways and think (and pay taxes) as industrial operators. They formed a Chamber of Commerce, jointly marketed Atuntaqui as a place of fashion, and opened bright new stores to the public. In one measure of their success, our 2005 survey of the sixty-eight sportswear producers (less than one-fourth of the estimated number of operations in Atuntaqui) revealed a workforce of 985, several hundred more than the old textile plant employed in its flush years.

Invasive Trades

Boom. Explosive growth. Boiling point. Writers have described trade surges as volatile upheavals that wipe out the old way of doing things. They have a point. We also have focused on the historic break that accompanies these commodity rushes. However, we have argued throughout this book that "invasive" is a more apt term. It captures the rupture, but, in borrowing from the idea of invasive species, the term suggests a longer evolution of these changes. The cases in this book point to four key moments: the disordering of a local economy; a critical innovation that often springs from a timely, well-matched arrival of an outsider; a smothering florescence; and then rapid development.

The prelude to invasion is more often than not disruption. The local economy has often fallen into disarray *before* the arrival of the new trade. Sometimes a boom elsewhere breaks the working heart of a provincial economy. When thousands left the countryside to work amid the petro-dollar prosperity of Quito in the 1970s, provincial lives morphed into national ones as country people found jobs in the capital, bought necessities in city marketplaces, and boarded interprovincial buses to shuttle between work and family. Other times, the disruption can start with a crisis. In Ecuador, national fiscal collapses in 1982 and again in 1999 led to devaluations of the currency and austere measures to pay down debt. The careers of men and women in Tigua, Otavalo, and Atuntaqui came to a standstill. As artisan production costs inflated, construction labor markets collapsed and the tourists stopped coming. Families watched their working and social capital drain away. Thus, the invasive dynamic is decidedly *not* the moment that capitalism itself arrives in some out-of-the-way place. Rather, it is when capitalism stumbles, when modern industrial enterprises run themselves into the ground, that conditions become ripe for an invasive trade. Having built—and then lost—a livelihood, men and women in the provinces stand willing to risk a lot on some new trade in order to recreate what they once thought they had.

An outside catalyst often jolts the trade into a new state of possibility. Sometimes an international actor makes a new connection between a product and an untapped market. With Tigua paintings, foreign-born gallery owners provided the reliable patronage to launch full-time artistic careers. Sweater makers had intermediaries from the United Kingdom or the United States who placed large orders and introduced new designs. Atuntaqui designers were local, but Colombian consultants arrived to teach about fashion seasons, sizing, and tailoring. Central American consultants came to arrange the machinery in the workshops.

However, we should be careful not to overstate the role of the outsider in contemporary invasive trades. In the 1920s, the construction of the Imbabura textile factory was all about the foreigner: the arrival of Spanish capital, English machines, Italian engineers, and a German manager. They invested vast resources, hired many laborers, and reaped profits for three decades. In the provincial trades that have launched since the 1970s, most of the skills, raw materials, and products already existed. In the case of the faja makers of Ariasucu, no one from outside the community helped. Homegrown innovation pushed the scale of production across a new threshold.

Then the boom. The ignition sequence has become predictable. An idiosyncratic product first offers part-time earnings for its creator, then becomes a full-time occupation, and then it is the public face of a town's economy. In home after home, low-cost machinery—retooled treadle looms, industrial sewing machines, or simple paint brushes—become as common as kitchen stoves. As an invasive trade takes over the local economy, waves of residents pile into the new trade. The first wave finds real earnings after the hard times caused by a fiscal crisis. The next wave picks up on the prosperity of these pioneers and copies their work. The third wave sees the huge success of the founder or a big reseller and finds an inexpensive, entry-level market niche to get a small part of the revenue (but then adds significantly to the volume). The next wave of households diverts earnings from other family enterprises to set themselves up as part timers. They accept low-margin work, perhaps at a loss, in the hope that they will not miss out on what has become the community's main source of cash. Just like the proverbial shovel merchants during a gold rush, the suppliers of raw material and machinery drive the expansion, often by offering creative credit terms. The once ordinary mix of businesses in a provincial city, or the diversified farming and wage jobs of a rural sector, disappear from view as the new businesses jockey for position with impressive displays of the town's new commodity.

Economic invasions rapidly evolve. The very producers who drive the boom often predict its quick ending. In Oaxaca, when the wood carving sales ramped up, there was a "widespread feeling during this time that the market might be short-lived" (Chibnik 2003, 39). Unprecedented in its growth and unmatched in the wealth it creates, the new business does not seem quite real. Sometimes innovation, boom, crisis, and yet another moment of economic disorder happen in quick succession. In Atuntaqui, the labor abuses and big-order fulfillment pressures invoked backlash both from within and outside the businesses. Within ten years of scaling up, firms laid off workers in big numbers.

It would be a mistake, though, to see Atuntaqui's retreat from large, local branded operations as a finale. The layoffs themselves did not terminate apparel production. They dispersed it through hundreds of new small family workshops that now climb their own ladder of artisan-like growth. Just as the Atuntaqui model was reaching its peak in 2005, the vice president of the Chamber of Commerce led a public relations firm on a tour of the old Imbabura textile factory. He wanted these Quito-based consultants to understand how important the upcoming trade show was. As they traversed the grounds around the plant, he said, "People look at Atuntaqui and the Expoferia trade show and they think this is something new, but that is not true. We have been *textileros* for eighty years." As the boom plays out and some of the branded operations wind down, Atuntaqui's neighborhoods fill with homegrown maquiladoras and Atuntaqui's streets fill with stores. The identity of being a textile worker has been renewed for another generation (see figure 33).

Thus, the larger point. Whatever the individual fortunes of the enterprises of an invasive economy, their investments build a collective legacy. The mass investment of personal effort saturates a community with new skills. Household workshops fill with similar toolkits. The fight for market share leaves behind

FIGURE 33. Teenage fashion shoot in the Imbabura textile factory for apparel maker CONGA's 2011 catalog (Photo credit: Albert Placencia, used by permission)

exhibition halls or galleries or remodeled plazas as well as all the private, branded stores. In a pure Ponzi scheme, the money is gone and the wealth evaporates in the liquidity of the early winners. In the speculative overreach of an artisan economy, the money forges an identity. It can materialize as an indigenous market plaza or peasant embroidery or native art or a fashionable T-shirt. The capital builds both an economic and cultural base to be tapped again.

So is an "invasive economy" another name for neoliberal capitalism playing out among artisans? In one sense, yes. Since the 1980s, "neoliberal" has been shorthand for a polarizing capitalism that combines the state's retreat from social welfare programs, its promotion of privatization, and its elevation of market relationships—regardless of social costs. To cope with austerity and the unwinding of state industries, new social policies promote individual competitiveness and entrepreneurship. Part-time work, street-selling, emigration, and informal labor markets have surged in response. The kind of artisan work discussed here, including belt weaving, sweater knitting, and indigenous painting, rapidly expanded, as individuals sought new trades to recover income and restore economic progress. As elsewhere in Latin America, the artisans responded as skilled neoliberal subjects: bootstrapping their own business out of their home, more often than not to get a piece of internationally connected commerce.

In another way, though, the making of contemporary artisan economies is about more than neoliberalism. At issue here is not just how pro-market, pro-capital policies have made working-class careers precarious, but what the role of mass production is in work, wealth, and social relations. This is the importance of the groundbreaking books of the 1980s. Piore and Sabel (1984), Lash and Urry (1987), and Harvey (1989) pointed out that the deindustrialization of advanced economies, which gained momentum in the 1970s, reopened basic questions of economics and society: how do communities of small producers share the costs of innovation and ensure that those who might lose from change will not be able to block it? In the absence of systematized and abstract prescriptions for development, how does a town learn practical lessons from its own popular and vernacular markets so as to expand opportunities? With the decline in industrial cities, how can the manufacturing that takes place on the periphery—in smaller towns and semirural areas—spark creativity and propel contemporary culture? Artisan production and the public economy it produces is the forum for debating and answering these questions.

Innovation, Inequality, and the Commons

In a sense, we are following the same path as some of the popular business writers and journalists we have distanced ourselves from, but in reverse. Concerned with the fate of a technology-driven, globally networked economy, Thomas Friedman, Adam Davidson, and Nassim Nicholas Taleb use artisans—or what they imagine artisans to be—as useful symbols. The autonomous craftsman stands for the human touch and a product individualized by the commitment of its maker. This version of the artisan is the opposite of scalable: artisan wares cannot be digitized; sales pitches are personal; the business platform is traditional tools and a hometown workshop. In this brewer-, baker-, cobbler-style artisan, the writers find authenticity, perseverance, or distinctiveness. And these qualities become part of the prescription for survival to be taken up by factory workers, managers, accountants, and other professionals whose jobs are jeopardized by global competition.

Having spent years researching and writing about actual artisans—painters and embroiderers and weavers and designers—we have seen the commitment to craft and quality that commentators celebrate. Yet for the rapidity of the economic changes we have seen, we often turn to treatises on digital commodities and economies to understand what is taking place among artisans. It should be obvious by now that the value of contemporary artisan work is fundamentally tied to innovation. More than that, contemporary artisans energetically innovate techniques that allow them to scale up. They simplify and standardize, moving from an older, body-powered apparatus to more productive machinery. Or they subdivide and routinize tasks, just as in Adam Smith's celebrated pin factory centuries ago.

The sequence of such changes can usefully be thought of as a series of acts that strip down the informational content of a commodity. Shedding the traditions at work in a product, artisans jettison the news they once bore when the very slant of the stitching revealed a mentor or the dimensions of a belt told of its home community. The disciplined course of innovation arrives at an object—a cotton shirt, a woven sash, a tourist painting, a sweater, or T-shirt—that is an extraordinarily efficient vehicle of the specific information that the average (uninformed) consumer will reward. These are garments as generic, open platforms of quickly produced and rapidly cycled designs: a llama or condor for those wanting Andeanness, Bob Marley for those needing a counterculture icon, or wolves and eagle feathers for those who want a New Age, indigenous aesthetic of nature. And in their simplicity, the new wares set up the most punishing form of competition. Their makers race so hard for sales partly because their once crafted trade goods have become basic commodities with little to distinguish them. Partly, they compete intensely because the informational content that could distinguish one product from its rivals spreads so easily. Skilled innovators that they are, today's home-based family manufacturers have achieved the nearly perfect open architecture of artisanal information transmission.

For all the openness, though, people copy unevenly. Sometimes someone is hit hard by it—for example, the rapid spread of the "face of the Indian" among acrylic sweater makers. At other times, in an open market plaza with scores of actively competing producers, some profitable designs are only copied by a portion of the market—for example, presidential embroidery. Sometimes a low-earning design will find a place in every stall and store, but another design that is a similarly reliable earner only has a following among a subset of producers. In these variations, the emergence of a design that truly stretches across all producers does not confirm the existence of a really profitable product. Rather, such an item is a particularly clear signal of a shared commitment to a common business. Where a profitable product design represents a successful variant in a class of goods that (temporarily) delivers earnings, the uniform design-in-common is an emblem of a longer-term, shared commitment of capital, time, and self. It symbolizes a durable site of productivity that lies beyond the current season's hot new product.

Ironically, having innovated in a way that eliminates so much of the individuality of their work, Andean artisans have arrived at a payoff structure akin to movie stars, the most individualized of contemporary global professionals. Furthermore, as with today's celebrities, self-making and culture-making go hand in hand. In the act of competing for attention and sales, shared expressive traditions—the symbols, codes, and habits that make lives intelligible and meaningful to each other—are co-opted by positional jockeying. Ultimately, in these artisan winner-take-all economies, the instruments that transfer value from the many to the few are cultural relations themselves. As these winners' incomes rise, neighbors closely attend to the habits and tastes of leaders, modeling their efforts on what seems to pay so handsomely. In quick order, the new producer feeds the wealth of the prosperous one—by providing goods to be resold, training workers who will move up, or recruiting customers who will move on to "the top" operation. Meanwhile, for those at the top, their earnings never free them from the effort to maintain their position. They may be the winners in the trade, but they are also creatures of it, duly bound to their artisan peers of all ranks.

Artisans still must live from the common value they create together. In our research, sometimes this collective value stood out most clearly when the community destroyed it. In the largest of Ecuador's artisan markets, Otavaleños entered a multiyear cycle of decline in the early 2000s. Price undercutting starved marginal earnings across numerous trades. Hiding designs and withdrawing from the plaza, producers muted the parade of colors and styles that visitors longed for in an open market. Those who did hustle for sales in the plaza were seen by other producers as the most likely to copy designs. Under these circumstances, artisans complained of their rivals' "disloyal competition." However, such accusations should not be read as Otavaleño intolerance for competition. Artisans accept and often even embrace competition. Many praise rivalry when they see that it expands their market. Thus, when speaking of disloyalty, they refer to pathology in the market, not to the market itself. The Otavaleño use of the term "competition" consequently raises an interesting question: if the opposite of disloyal competition is not "no competition" but "loyal competition," what are competitors loyal to?

At meetings of cooperatives, artisan unions, and chambers of commerce in Otavalo, Tigua, and Atuntaqui there is a glimpse of an answer: "loyalty" is the moral consciousness that ensures the viability of a trade. At gatherings of tradespeople in Otavalo, some insist that public investment must create an "economy with identity." In Atuntaqui, workshop owners want quality improvement programs for individual plants and a local seal of quality that includes them all. Still others in both the indigenous marketplace and the old factory town want an annual civic festival to be promoted to national audiences so that the flow of customers grows. Through such demands, the producers hope to build a set of joint resources: cultural heritage, a professional reputation, and the commercial appeal of their hometown.

These are the cultural commons intrinsic to contemporary artisan commerce. The use of "commons" here is not just a metaphor. Small, household-based manufacturers work through formal organizations to protect and regulate pooled resources. They grapple with the rules of community governance: how to define membership in their trade, how to keep powerful outsiders at bay, how to allot contributions for annual events, and how to increase market access so that a new generation has opportunity.

Some of what they protect has been handed down to them from parents and grandparents. Much, though, has been generated by today's operators, not just through their own innovations, but as a cumulative consequence of their competition with each other. If few intended to share the value of their efforts with others, such value nonetheless becomes an object of explicit concern. The skilled embroiderer Teresa Casa epitomizes the kind of "commons consciousness" these artisan marketplaces engender. Presented with the knockoffs of her designs, she is both annoyed at the copies and proud that she has contributed to business, a craft she credits to her mother's generation and work she believes is essential for other women like her. Her career blends entrepreneurship and guardianship—she connects, but does not merge, the "I" of her workshop to the "we" of her people.

The Artisan Public Economy

Adam Smith's famous example of the pin factory seems very familiar to us: a poorly capitalized operation with laborers picking up several tasks as they break down an old craft trade into new jobs and expanded production. In the northern Andes we have seen a number of communities and trades go through this sequence. But we refer to Smith for more than ethnographic reasons. Impressed by the economic power of specialization, Smith was aware of a fundamental problem. As commerce grows, as manufactories dissolve craftsmanship, as each person specializes in a single product or even a piece of a product, each individual becomes increasingly dependent on others. Self-sufficiency perishes; each person "has almost constant occasion for the help of his brethren" (Smith 1981 [1776], 1: 18). Yet, even though everyone is beholden in this way, "it is vain for him to expect [help] from their benevolence only" (1981, 1: 18).

Smith outlined the argument that the market solves the problem. Individual interest in personal gain induces each to the most profitable trades, occupations that derive economic value from meeting unmet needs. Thus the famous "invisible hand": the profit-seeking merchant promotes the interests of society better than if he had actually intended to do so. The pin maker will thus not want for meat, nor the butcher for cloth, nor the weaver for pins as each sells and then buys, and thus each provides and receives "help." In Smith's account, though, it is not just the benevolent, guiding hand that is invisible. So are all the rivals. If faja weaving or T-shirt making are anything to go by, the business you are most likely to encounter upon stepping out of your pin factory is another pin factory. This neighboring enterprise is likely the one to steal your client. It is also the one that most completely understands your problems. And as this pin-making peer goes about her work, she solves issues with suppliers and workers and customers, solutions that will set the parameters for your efforts as well.

Smith's most commonly cited passages drop such mutuality. They celebrate instead specialization and the power of self-interested exchange. Productivity and efficiency become *the* promise of the free market. In contrast, with an extended examination of invasive trades, this book focuses not on differentiation among forms of work, but the multiplication of the same kind of work. And by making the wider business visible, we underscore what is missing in the popularization of Smith's ideas: the potency of the shared base built up by a set of producers. More to the point, we argue for fundamentally expanding our thinking about the sources of help in an open marketplace. Indeed, along with Smith, we find that manufacturers can build much shared value without intending to do so. However, producers are people, not abstract economic actors. They have parents whom they hope to do proud and children whose careers they want to help launch. They seek the respect of their neighbors, bear grudges, and feel an obligation to a community. All of this pushes people to engage with each other as more than vendors and customers. Amid the growing consciousness of connectedness comes a bigger push for cooperation.

In chapter 5, we described the decline of a large textile factory and argued that real success came to Atuntaqui with the rise of a new public economy. The hidden household-based manufacturers, secret designs, and private sales spilled out into the light of day. Business owners pursued a wider civic vision as part of building their enterprises. Not everyone agreed with this approach. Debate ensued. Town authorities curtailed the textile operators. Some projects passed from private hands to municipal employees, and eventually to the heritage experts employed by the national government. Even in disagreement, though, the early discussions widened the cultural stakes and scope of civic business in Atuntaqui. Then the economic problems began to stack up, the textile cluster model faltered, and the entrepreneurs withdrew again, deflating the new civic spirit.

The public moment may have been too brief and too fragile, but it did indicate the possibility of transforming an older artisan tradition into something vibrant. A similar civic opening has persisted in Otavalo as artisans and others push for the future of an economy with identity.

Artisan Prescriptions

Throughout this book, we have challenged the artisan-invoking economic prescriptions that crop up on op-ed pages in the United States. Such descriptions of artisans did not ring true to us. Having now laid out the artisan industries, the innovations, the setbacks, the common value, and the public life of an artisan economy, we will honor these other writers with an effort to offer our own prescriptions. Among the lessons that may be taken from artisan economies in the northern Andes are the following:

1. As a promising, place-based local manufactory springs up, cast a wide net and do not overlook agriculture, farms, food, and risk-ready operators in the countryside. In the United States the matching of new farmers markets with urban revitalization efforts resonates with the long-standing provincial weekly markets of South America. Especially in regions where agriculture once offered significant employment, linking artisan economies with farms and food diversifies the economy and connects to histories of place, even if it does not deliver immediate or outsize profits.

2. Even if one sector seems to be delivering wider benefits and seems to be civic-minded, be wary about resentment if that sector ap-

pears to be privatizing public resources. At the same time, do not assume that a successful sector always delivers profit for those most engaged in it.

3. Always keep in mind the possibility of artisan bid-down. Indeed, if proprietors keep piling into a signature trade, the apparent vitality of a place-based vocation will come to hide the meager earnings it delivers to any one member. Absent any effort to defend the sustainability of a market, competitors undercut prices and drive earnings down to what amounts to subsistence wages. Although this is standard advice for competing with far-flung producers in a global economy, local economies are vulnerable to the same bid-down. As Ecuadorian producers constantly worried about low-cost imports from Asia or other Latin American countries, they missed the low-cost competition just down the street.

4. In phases of destructive competition, the retreat from public life does not solve the structural problems of a trade. Hiding one's operation may not even return an individual firm to profitability. Businesses may defend a few exclusive designs at the expense of developing their creative capacity, or come to depend on a few clients at the cost of widening their customer base. Their operations become more vulnerable in the process.

5. Community projects must find a popular angle; cultural heritage and patrimony efforts must be inclusive. Beware narrow and technical takeovers in the name of preservation and expertise.

6. When it comes to fairness in the marketplace, think in terms of generations. Rather than exploitative relations, sometimes extraordinary profits reflect new realities of connectivity, networks, or the concentration of rewards through a few deep-pocket buyers. However, in artisan trades that draw on community traditions, it is reasonable to challenge the privileged, ask them to justify their earnings, and remedy the monopolization of joint resources. Often common ground among the successful and the struggling is found in the necessity of maintaining real opportunity for new entrants.

This last point is more of a starting point than a final observation. Closely examining these Andean marketplaces provides timely lessons in the workings of careers in contemporary capitalism, including the necessity of skilled work, innovation, and finding an edge. But when those careers get traction, the crucial tasks lie just beyond the boundary of an enterprise. Rather quickly, a group of competitors will launch a new commons of ideas, culture, and value. The terms in which they recognize their shared ground and the ways they come to care for it are among the most interesting and important lessons to be learned from contemporary artisans.

Notes

PROLOGUE

1. All translations ours unless otherwise noted.

2. In some ways both the Ecuadorian and Colombian plans for development are constrained by their positions within a global system in which "capital accumulation moves from Fordist, verticalized processes to a division between financial hubs and proliferating flexible (post-Fordist) subcontracting and outsourcing units, a process that increasingly saturates all sectors of the social order, not least the state itself" (Friedman and Ekholm Friedman 2013, 248). These movements and trends in capital accumulation need to be considered, but they do not entirely determine either national or regional responses, as is shown in these northern Andean case studies. We discuss these ideas further in the book's conclusion.

3. In a March 7, 2011, blog post on *The Discipline of Innovation*, Tim Kastelle showcases the Otavalo Mountain Shirt as "Innovation Lessons from J. Peterman" and writes that Peterman made the great discovery of "selling stories." Indeed.

CHAPTER I

1. The anthropologists Jonathan Friedman and Kajsa Ekholm Friedman comment perceptively that "the spiral of violent conflicts and now-rolling crises that began in the United States and have spread to Europe has made it difficult to maintain globalized optimism. For advocates of

globalization discourse, all of this is something of a tragedy" (2013, 246). This description is certainly appropriate for the trajectory of Thomas Friedman's writing. In an ironic nod, Friedman and Ekholm Friedman call Thomas Friedman "that other Friedman" (2013, 251).

2. For a recent comparison retracing some of these ideas, see economist Robert H. Frank on *The Darwin Economy* (2011). Frank's headline is that Charles Darwin more accurately described the potential downsides of competition than Adam Smith did, but what the book reveals is more how Darwin was influenced by philosophers like Smith and how ideas about the effects of mechanistic competition in both the human economy and natural world were intertwined at the time (Frank 2011, 18).

3. Michael Chibnik's (2011, 118–41) discussion of "Who Makes Household Economic Decisions?" is pertinent. Artisans often pool resources and decision making at the household level. However, within the household there can also be a great deal of disagreement, fragmentation, and pursuit of autonomy. Then there is the added conundrum of trying to define household boundaries and membership, especially when household and business overlap as when the household becomes a primary site for producing marketable commodities.

CHAPTER 2

1. For a more extended analysis, see "Peasants and *Pirámides*: Consumer Fantasies in the Colombian Andes" (Antrosio 2012). The information on peasant agriculture transformations and the appropriation of consumer items is from *Todo Moderno: Significados de la modernización en la Sierra colombiana* (Antrosio 2008).

2. Rudi Colloredo-Mansfeld's first book *The Native Leisure Class: Consumption and Cultural Creativity in the Andes* (1999) opens with the story of fattening two pigs and trying to sell them before a potential price collapse.

3. Enrique Mayer and Manuel Glave documented similar market calculations in Peru. During most periods only the wealthier peasants can afford to grow potatoes for household consumption (1999). Most others will sell their home-grown potatoes, or at least sell the biggest and best of the home-grown potatoes, and then buy cheaper ones in the market plaza.

4. We analyze this dynamic further in chapter 3, noting how winner-

take-all competition can sustain artisan production. Although it is impossible to reconstruct the precise dynamic of potato production in the 1950s and 1960s, there are strong hints that it followed a logic of an invasive trade, with some dramatic early wins creating a piling-on effect, and then routinizing as a tradition in these historically invaded communities.

5. There is an interesting contrast between how John Comaroff and Jean Comaroff (2009) treat corporations in *Ethnicity, Inc.* and how Torres sees corporations as part of a deeply rooted history of peasant engagement. However, the contrast may be partly a consequence of tone, style, and emphasis. The Comaroffs emphasize newness while leaving open the possibility of historical depth: "Could it be that we are seeing unfold before us a metamorphosis in the production of identity and subjectivity, in the politics and economics of culture and, concomitantly, in the ontology of ethnic consciousness? Or are we merely witness to the intensification of something that has been around for a long time, something immanent hiding in the half-light of the convoluted, often unexpected history of capitalism, something now being forced fully into view? Are both things possible?" (2009, 21).

6. Michael Kearney's (1996) *Reconceptualizing the Peasantry* became a classic example of defining peasants by percentage of resources devoted to subsistence. This definition made it possible for Kearney to claim that peasants were "mostly gone and that global conditions do not favor the perpetuation of those who remain" (3).

7. For more references to the anthropological literature see an earlier version of this chapter published as "Risk-Seeking Peasants, Excessive Artisans: Speculation in the Northern Andes" (Antrosio and Colloredo-Mansfeld 2014).

8. Henrich and McElreath say their economic games resemble "actual cropping decisions" in terms of how "farmers often face a choice between their traditional seed (which approximates a 'sure thing') and high-tech seed that may produce a higher yield (higher gain) but, if not dealt with properly, may yield substantially less. Sowing either seed will provide a 'gain' relative to not planting (even in a bad year, fields usually yield something)" (2002, 179). These assertions are at odds with the ethnographic evidence presented here. First, traditional seeds do not approximate sure things. Second, yielding "something" in a bad year is not necessarily a gain, when all the costs are factored. As Mayer and

Glave demonstrated empirically, peasant production is often premised on not factoring in these costs (1999). Finally, drawing the line between the traditional and the high-tech is not always easy—peasants have been experimenting with different seeds and techniques for many years. As Chibnik puts it, these are "experiments that diverge too much from real-life situations to be of much use in understanding social norms" (2011, 117).

9. Lehmann tracked a common transaction in the northern Andes that could be technically translated as "sharecropping"—crop agreements in which one person provides the land and one provides the seed—and has therefore been seen as a traditional arrangement akin to an imagined feudal hacienda. Lehmann discovered these were actually sophisticated systems of short-term contracts. "The idea that sharecropping is a contract between a richer partner who owns the land and a poorer one who is landless receives very little support from our data.... The contracts have forced us to write of sharecropping in this context as a capitalist partnership rather than as a form of tenancy" (1986a, 342, 351).

10. We concur with Michael Chibnik's recent assessment regarding the difficulties in defining risk and uncertainty: "Economists and psychologists writing about risk and uncertainty usually devote only a paragraph or two to the relevance of their models and experiments to on-the-ground decision making. They rarely discuss multiple risks and uncertainties, choices that fall along a fuzzy risk-uncertainty continuum, hard-to-measure and often incommensurable costs and benefits, and conflicting short-term and long-term payoffs from decisions" (2011, 88).

11. Chibnik would basically agree with Reinhardt that "long-established ('traditional') subsistence crops are often less risky than agricultural products sold at markets. Time-tested varieties of staple crops usually provide adequate yields in varying environmental conditions. Cash crops, in contrast, may be recent introductions to an area that is subject to blights and provide good yields only in optimal growing conditions" (Chibnik 2011, 49). This may to a certain extent be true, except that many of the crops that seem to be "traditional" subsistence crops in the northern Andes—potatoes, beans, cabbage, corn—have been intertwined with hybrid varieties and markets for at least fifty years.

CHAPTER 3

1. Our analysis parallels those who see contemporary globalization as a specific phase within a previously established global system. There are observable trends in production patterns and identity, but this is certainly not the first arrival of capitalism (see chapter 2; Friedman and Ekholm Friedman 2013; Trouillot 2003).

2. The growth in Ariasucu echoed the weaving trades in Guatemala that likewise profited when rural indigenous peoples forsook subsistence autonomy for wage work, urban residences, and other opportunities for cash incomes and consumer goods (Smith 1978, 1984a).

3. Analysis of twenty years of purchases among Ariasucu households suggests that consumer good accumulation serves as a good proxy for income. The annual rate of accumulation varies with income—during years of low earnings, purchases drop off (see Colloredo-Mansfeld 1999, fig. 8, 141). Moreover, proprietors of faja weaving operations expressed similar spending priorities, in terms of building a house or accumulating consumer goods to furnish it. That is, none of the weavers seemed to be accumulating goods or a car in lieu of housing investments that might make one operation's earnings seem artificially low relative to others. However, among non-weavers, especially young handicraft dealers, values ranged widely concerning the relative importance of modern consumer goods as compared to house-building.

4. At these wages people deemed painting comparable to and substitutable for other employment, such as working on commercial potato farms, apprenticing in mechanic shops, or loading cargo at the bus terminal. In other words, they saw no economic advantage to painting, but rather chose to paint because it was "softer" work, because it allowed them to work in their own homes, or because they took pride in it as "our own" indigenous work.

5. To be among the fourteen "first-rank" artists identified by their peers, painters must contribute to the development of Tigua art, demonstrate creative flair, and maintain consistent sales. From the perspective of gallery purchases, eleven individuals stand out for authoring 10 percent or more of any single inventory; sixteen find their work purchased by more than one gallery. It should be noted that being both a producer and intermediary can be a mark of success in Andean agriculture as well (see chapter 2).

6. In this sense, the accusations of drug running, levied against

sweater merchants from Otavalo and potato growers in Túquerres, seem quite similar to older accusations of devil pacts—that the wealthy made pacts with the devil to become rich. Michael Taussig's (1980) famous analysis in *The Devil and Commodity Fetishism in South America* was that the devil pacts represented a capitalist mentality as opposed to a peasant subsistence mentality (see also chapter 2). Our account here indicates instead that such accusations are usually intracommunity, or within market-capitalist relationships. As Trouillot put it: "The key contradiction in the society under study may not be between capitalism and a bucolic pre-Conquest world, but may lie within capitalism itself—or more precisely in the very fact that any economic 'system' manifests itself in real life only through the actions of individuals who do not necessarily care about its abstract 'logic'" (1986, 88; see also Edelman 1994).

7. The other strange part of this denouncing exercise is that among anthropological insiders the term "neoliberal" became a kind of curseword invective, automatically associated with evil capitalist activities. Meanwhile, outsiders to anthropology (especially in the United States) often did not know what anthropologists were talking about, in part because it was not always clear that the neoliberal reforms were actually what most people would consider a *conservative*, promarket approach. See Julia Elyachar (2012) for more on the use of neoliberalism as an epithet and see Daniel Mains (2012) for an argument against further use of neoliberalism as an analytical category.

8. Economic anthropologist Stuart Plattner is one of the few to explore the issues of winner-take-all economics in the United States. In an ethnography of the St. Louis art market, he considers how markets allocate rewards when earnings bear little obvious relation to either production costs or talent. His analysis emphasizes the power of one locale (New York) to define what is significant in the art world and "the social construction of fine-art value that makes the social setting of a work paramount over its physical characteristics" (1996, 8).

9. Since 1990, more than a dozen exhibitions of Tigua art have been held in university museums, fine "folk art" galleries, and elsewhere in Ecuador, the United States, Canada, and Europe. Books related to two exhibitions have been published featuring the founder Julio Toaquiza and his family (Colvin and Toaquiza 1995; Ribadeneira de Casares 1990)

10. Indeed, in 1999, getting a Julio Toaquiza painting required noth-

ing more than $24 and the patience to shuffle through a stack of sixty anonymous paintings in a mid-range Quiteño gallery.

11. This is clearest when Taleb turns directly to Friedman, saying "he promoted the 'earth is flat' idea of globalization without realizing that globalization brings fragilities, causes more extreme events as a side effect, and requires a great deal of redundancies to operate properly" (2012, 384). And even though Friedman was wrong "the problem is that the journalist Thomas Friedman is still driving the bus. There is no penalty for opinion makers who harm society. And this is a very bad practice" (2012, 384).

CHAPTER 4

1. Indeed, Lessig himself worries about the ways corporations and individuals have extended intellectual property law to undermine the freedom of the Internet. For a more recent ethnography of hackers, Gabriella Coleman's *Coding Freedom* (2013) traces similar themes regarding a collective enterprise built on an individualistic ethos.

2. Michael Chibnik noted similar variation with regard to wood carvers in Oaxaca: "The decisions that . . . Oaxacan wood carvers have made about openness and secrecy illustrate well the multiple risks and uncertainties associated with many choices about cooperation and competition. Artisans sharing a particular innovation cannot predict the economic effects of their generosity" (2011, 98). This seems certainly true for artisans in Otavalo, where neither secrecy nor openness guaranteed success.

3. In our original analysis, we worked with anthropologist Eric C. Jones to undertake social network analysis of the study as a two-mode data set (Colloredo-Mansfeld, Antrosio, and Jones 2011). In that analysis, we were able to show how producers differentiated themselves by the types and number of designs they brought to market. However, with thirty producers displaying eighteen designs over the course of eighteen months, the visualizations we generated became too dense and the changes too difficult to discern. As an alternative, we have hand drawn the sequences to show the way producers connect through four details: hand embroidery, appliqué, sequins, and presidential embroidery. The renderings are a small act of handwork solidarity with the artisans we report on here.

4. This point corresponds with observations in chapter 3 that winner-

take-all competition or even artisan profits cannot always be directly tied to capital accumulation.

5. We adapted this survey from work done by Hirschfeld (1977) on Cuna Molas.

6. For these producers, the correlation coefficient between their preference scores and their fashion scores is .916 and is significant at the .001 level using Spearman's rho. In contrast, the relationship between cultural value and preference is negligible.

7. T stat = −2.84, p <.05.

8. T stat = 2.094, p <.05.

9. The correlation was .509, p <.001.

10. Spearman's rho .920, p <.01.

CHAPTER 5

1. The literature on clusters became vast, like a cluster of its own for the business and development world. The article by Ron Martin and Peter Sunley, "Deconstructing Clusters: Chaotic Concept or Policy Panacea?" (2003) is a helpful review of the fad. In a more academic and economic treatment, Philip McCann and Stephen Sheppard's "The Rise, Fall and Rise Again of Industrial Location Theory" (2003) discusses how ideas like Michael Porter's industrial cluster surged without paying enough attention to the previous attempts—and insoluble problems—to understand how and why industries appear to grow in particular regions. Interestingly, Porter's idea of securing competitive advantage through clusters experienced its own rise and fall in the last decade. Porter founded Monitor, a consulting group, which at its height was seen as offering premier and thoughtful business strategy. Porter moved on, and while Porter remains at the Harvard Business School, the Monitor consulting group he cofounded went bankrupt in 2012.

Bibliography

Acheson, James M. 1988. *The Lobster Gangs of Maine*. Hanover, NH: University Press of New England.

Agrawal, Arun. 2003. "Sustainable Governance of Common-Pool Resources: Context, Methods, and Politics." *Annual Review of Anthropology* 32 (1): 243–62.

Annis, Sheldon. 1987. *God and Production in a Guatemalan Town*. Austin: University of Texas Press.

Antrosio, Jason. 2008. *Todo Moderno: Significados de la Modernización en la Sierra Colombiana*. Quito, Ecuador: Abya-Yala.

———. 2012. "Peasants and *Pirámides*: Consumer Fantasies in the Colombian Andes." In *Consumer Culture in Latin America*, edited by Anna Cristina Pertierra and John Sinclair, 81–92. New York: Palgrave Macmillan.

Antrosio, Jason, and Rudi Colloredo-Mansfeld. 2014. "Risk-Seeking Peasants, Excessive Artisans: Speculation in the Northern Andes." *Economic Anthropology* 1 (1): 124–38.

Arthur, W. Brian. 2005. "The Logic of Invention." *Santa Fe Institute Working Paper 05-12-045*, December 19.

Barrère, Christian, and Sophie Delabruyère. 2011. "Intellectual Property Rights on Creativity and Heritage: The Case of the Fashion Industry." *European Journal of Law and Economics* 32 (3): 305–39.

Bateson, Gregory. 1972. *Steps to an Ecology of Mind*. Chicago: University of Chicago Press.

Bebbington, Anthony. 2004. "Social Capital and Development Studies 1: Critique, Debate, Progress?" *Progress in Development Studies* 4 (4): 343–49.

Bonilla, Adrián, and César Montúfar. 2008. "Two Perspectives on Ecuador: Rafael Correa's Political Project." *Inter-American Dialog: Working Paper Series* August: 1–16.

Bourdieu, Pierre. 1986. "The Forms of Capital." In *Handbook of Theory and Research for the Sociology of Education*, edited by John G. Richardson, 241–58. New York: Greenwood Press.

———. 1993. *The Field of Cultural Production: Essays on Art and Literature.* New York: Columbia University Press.

Braudel, Fernand. 1982. *Civilization and Capitalism, 15th–18th Century.* Translated by Sian Reynolds. Vol. 2, *The Wheels of Commerce.* New York: Harper & Row.

Brulotte, Ronda L. 2012. *Between Art and Artifact: Archaeological Replicas and Cultural Production in Oaxaca Mexico.* Austin: University of Texas Press.

Bruno, John F., Coleman W. Kennedy, Tatyana A. Rand, and Mary-Bestor Grant. 2004. "Landscape-Scale Patterns of Biological Invasions in Shoreline Plant Communities." *Oikos* 107 (3): 531–40.

Burt, Ronald S. 1992. *Structural Holes: The Social Structure of Competition.* Cambridge, MA: Harvard University Press.

Cahill, David. 2010. "Advanced Andeans and Backward Europeans: Structure and Agency in the Collapse of the Inca Empire." In *Questioning Collapse: Human Resilience, Ecological Vulnerability, and the Aftermath of Empire*, edited by Patricia A. McAnany and Norman Yoffee. New York: Cambridge University Press.

Chan, Anita Say. 2011. "Competitive Tradition: Intellectual Property and New Millennial Craft." *Anthropology of Work Review* 32 (2): 90–102.

Chen, Tina Mai. 2001. "Dressing for the Party: Clothing, Citizenship, and Gender-Formation in Mao's China." *Fashion Theory: The Journal of Dress, Body & Culture* 5 (2): 143–71.

Chevalier, Jacques M. 1982. *Civilization and the Stolen Gift: Capital, Kin, and Cult in Eastern Peru.* Toronto: University of Toronto Press.

———. 1983. "There Is Nothing Simple about Simple Commodity Production." *Journal of Peasant Studies* 10 (4): 153–86.

Chibnik, Michael. 2003. *Crafting Tradition: The Making and Marketing of Oaxacan Wood Carvings.* Austin: University of Texas Press.

———. 2011. *Anthropology, Economics, and Choice.* Austin: University of Texas Press.

Christensen, Clayton M. 1997. *The Innovator's Dilemma: When New Technologies Cause Great Firms to Fail.* Cambridge, MA: Harvard Business Review Press.

Clark, Gracia. 1994. *Onions Are My Husband: Survival and Accumulation by West African Market Women.* Chicago: University of Chicago Press.

———. 1999. "Mothering, Work, and Gender in Urban Asante Ideology and Practice." *American Anthropologist* 101 (4): 717–29.

Coleman, E. Gabriella. 2013. *Coding Freedom: The Ethics and Aesthetics of Hacking.* Princeton: Princeton University Press.

Coleman, James S. 1988. "Social Capital in the Creation of Human Capital." *American Journal of Sociology* 94 (Supplement): S95–S120.

Colloredo-Mansfeld, Rudi. 1999. *The Native Leisure Class: Consumption and Cultural Creativity in the Andes.* Chicago: University of Chicago Press.

———. 2002. "An Ethnography of Neoliberalism: Understanding Competition in Artisan Economies." *Current Anthropology* 43 (1): 113–37.

———. 2009. *Fighting Like a Community: Andean Civil Society in an Era of Indian Uprisings.* Chicago: University of Chicago Press.

Colloredo-Mansfeld, Rudi, and Jason Antrosio. 2009. "Economic Clusters or Cultural Commons? The Limits of Competition-Driven Development in the Ecuadorian Andes." *Latin American Research Review* 44 (1): 132–57.

———. 2012. "Economías Públicas y Escondidas en Atuntaqui (Ecuador): los Desafíos de la Cooperación Sostenible en la Producción." *Eutopía* 3: 69–92.

Colloredo-Mansfeld, Rudi, Jason Antrosio, and Eric C. Jones. 2011. "Creativity, Place, and Commodities: The Making of Public Economies in Andean Apparel Industries." In *Textile Economies: Power and Value from the Local to the Transnational,* edited by Walter E. Little and Patricia A. McAnany, 39–55. Lanham, MD: AltaMira Press.

Colloredo-Mansfeld, Rudi, Paola Mantilla, and Jason Antrosio. 2012. "Rafael Correa's Multicolored Dream Shirt: Commerce, Creativity, and National Identity in Post-Neoliberal Ecuador." *Latin American and Caribbean Ethnic Studies* 7 (3): 275–94.

Colvin, Jean, and Alfredo Toaquiza. 1995. *Pintores de Tigua: Indigenous Artists of Ecuador.* Quito: Libri Mundi.

Comaroff, John L., and Jean Comaroff. 2009. *Ethnicity, Inc.* Chicago: University of Chicago Press.

Cook, Scott. 1986. "The 'Managerial' vs. the 'Labor' Function, Capital Accumulation, and the Dynamics of Simple Commodity Production in Rural Oaxaca, Mexico." In *Entrepreneurship and Social Change*, edited by Sidney M. Greenfield and Arnold Strickon, 54–95. Lanham, MD: University Press of America.

———. 1998. *Mexican Brick Culture in the Building of Texas, 1800s–1980s.* College Station: Texas A&M University Press.

Cook, Scott, and Leigh Binford. 1990. *Obliging Need: Rural Petty Industry in Mexican Capitalism.* Austin: University of Texas Press.

Costin, Cathy Lynne. 1998. "Housewives, Chosen Women, Skilled Men: Cloth Production and Social Identity in the Late Prehispanic Andes." *Archeological Papers of the American Anthropological Association* 8 (1): 123–41.

Crow, Joanna. 2010. "Introduction: Intellectuals, Indigenous Ethnicity and the State in Latin America." *Latin American and Caribbean Ethnic Studies* 5 (2): 99–107.

de Janvry, Alain. 1981. *The Agrarian Question and Reformism in Latin America.* Baltimore: Johns Hopkins University Press.

Departamento Nacional de Planeación. 2011. Plan Nacional de Desarrollo 2010–2014: "Prosperidad para Todos" Resumen Ejecutivo. Bogotá, Colombia.

Durkheim, Emile. 1984 [1893]. *The Division of Labor in Society.* Translated by W. D. Halls. New York: Macmillan.

Dyer, Jeff, Hal Gregersen, and Clayton M. Christensen. 2011. *The Innovator's DNA: Mastering the Five Skills of Disruptive Innovators.* Cambridge, MA: Harvard Business Review Press.

Edelman, Marc. 1994. "Landlords and the Devil: Class, Ethnic, and Gender Dimensions of Central American Peasant Narratives." *Cultural Anthropology* 9 (1): 58–93.

Eglash, Ron. 1999. *African Fractals: Modern Computing and Indigenous Design.* New Brunswick, NJ: Rutgers University Press.

Elton, Charles S. 1958. *The Ecology of Invasions by Animals and Plants.* London: Methuen.

Elyachar, Julia. 2012. "Before (and after) Neoliberalism: Tacit Knowledge, Secrets of the Trade, and the Public Sector in Egypt." *Cultural Anthropology* 27 (1): 76–96.

Evans, Philip, and Thomas S. Wurster. 2000. *Blown to Bits: How the*

New Economics of Information Transforms Strategy. Boston: Harvard Business School Press.

Femenías, Blenda. 2004. *Gender and the Boundaries of Dress in Contemporary Peru*. Austin: University of Texas Press.

Fine, Ben. 2001. *Social Capital Versus Social Theory: Political Economy and Social Science at the Turn of the Millennium*. New York: Routledge.

Frank, Robert H. 1999. *Luxury Fever: Why Money Fails to Satisfy in an Era of Excess*. New York: The Free Press.

———. 2011. *The Darwin Economy: Liberty, Competition, and the Common Good*. Princeton: Princeton University Press.

Frank, Robert H., and Philip J. Cook. 1995. *The Winner-Take-All Society: Why the Few at the Top Get So Much More Than the Rest of Us*. New York: Penguin.

Freeman, Richard B. 2008. "Why Do We Work More Than Keynes Expected?" In *Revisiting Keynes: Economic Possibilities for Our Grandchildren*, edited by Lorenzo Pecchi and Gustavo Piga, 135–42. Cambridge, MA: MIT Press.

Friedman, Jonathan, and Kajsa Ekholm Friedman. 2013. "Globalization as a Discourse of Hegemonic Crisis: A Global Systemic Analysis." *American Ethnologist* 40 (2): 244–57.

Friedman, Thomas L., and Michael Mandelbaum. 2011. *That Used to Be Us: How America Fell Behind in the World It Invented and How We Can Come Back*. New York: Farrar, Straus and Giroux.

Friedmann, Harriet. 1978. "World Market, State and Family Farm: Social Bases of Household Production in the Era of Wage Labor." *Comparative Studies in Society and History* 20 (4): 545–86.

Geertz, Clifford. 1973. *The Interpretation of Cultures*. New York: Basic Books.

Gibson-Graham, J. K. 1996. *The End of Capitalism (As We Knew It): A Feminist Critique of Political Economy*. Oxford: Blackwell Publishers.

———. 2006. *A Postcapitalist Politics*. Minneapolis: University of Minnesota Press.

Gudeman, Stephen. 2001. *The Anthropology of Economy: Community, Market, and Culture*. Malden, MA: Wiley-Blackwell.

———. 2005. "Community and Economy: Economy's Base." In *A Handbook of Economic Anthropology*, edited by James G. Carrier, 94–106. Northampton, MA: Edward Elgar Publishing.

Habermas, Jurgen. 1989. "The Public Sphere." In *Jurgen Habermas on*

Society and Politics: A Reader, edited by Steven Seidman, 231–36. Boston: Beacon Press.

Hardin, Garrett. 1968. "The Tragedy of the Commons." *Science* 162 (3859): 1243–48.

Harvey, David. 1989. *The Condition of Postmodernity*. Oxford: Blackwell Publishers.

Heard, Matthew J., Dov F. Sax, and John F. Bruno. 2012. "Dominance of Non-Native Species Increases over Time in a Historically Invaded Strandline Community." *Diversity and Distributions* 18 (12): 1232–42.

Henrich, Joseph, and Richard McElreath. 2002. "Are Peasants Risk-Averse Decision Makers?" *Current Anthropology* 43 (1): 172–81.

Hippel, Eric von. 2005. *Democratizing Innovation*. Cambridge, MA: MIT Press.

Hirschfeld, Lawrence A. 1977. "Cuna Aesthetics: A Quantitative Analysis." *Ethnology* 16 (2): 147–66.

Howard, Rosaleen. 2010. "Language, Signs, and the Performance of Power: The Discursive Struggle over Decolonization in the Bolivia of Evo Morales." *Latin American Perspectives* 37 (3): 176–94.

Hyde, Lewis. 2010. *Common as Air: Revolution, Art, and Ownership*. New York: Farrar, Straus and Giroux.

Ingold, Tim. 2000. *The Perception of the Environment: Essays on Livelihood, Dwelling and Skill*. London: Routledge.

———. 2013. *Making: Anthropology, Archaeology, Art and Architecture*. New York: Routledge.

Jackson, Michael. 1998. *Minima Ethnographica: Intersubjectivity and the Anthropological Project*. Chicago: University of Chicago Press.

Johnson, Allen W. 1971. *Sharecroppers of the Sertão: Economics and Dependence on a Brazilian Plantation*. Stanford: Stanford University Press.

Kahn, Joel S. 1980. *Minangkabau Social Formations: Indonesian Peasants and the World-Economy*. New York: Cambridge University Press.

Kearney, Michael. 1996. *Reconceptualizing the Peasantry*. Boulder, CO: Westview Press.

Kelty, Christopher M. 2008. *Two Bits: The Cultural Significance of Free Software*. Durham: Duke University Press.

Kintto, Lucas. 2007. "New Ecuadorian President Calls for '21st Century Socialism.'" *The Global Report* 419: 1.

Kirshenblatt-Gimblett, Barbara. 1998. *Destination Culture: Tourism, Museums, and Heritage*. Berkeley: University of California Press.

Lalander, Rickard. 2009. "Los Indígenas y la Revolución Ciudadana:

Rupturas y Alianzas en Cotacachi y Otavalo." *Ecuador Debate* 77: 185–218.

Lash, Scott, and John Urry. 1987. *The End of Organized Capitalism.* Madison: University of Wisconsin Press.

Lazear, Edward P., and Sherwin Rosen. 1981. "Rank-Order Tournaments as Optimum Labor Contracts." *Journal of Political Economy* 89 (5): 841–64.

Lehmann, David. 1986a. "Sharecropping and the Capitalist Transition in Agriculture." *Journal of Development Economics* 23 (2): 333–54.

———. 1986b. "Two Paths of Agrarian Capitalism, or a Critique of Chayanovian Marxism." *Comparative Studies in Society and History* 28 (4): 601–27.

Leijonhufvud, Axel. 2008. "Spreading the Bread Thin on the Butter." In *Revisiting Keynes: Economic Possibilities for Our Grandchildren*, edited by Lorenzo Pecchi and Gustavo Piga, 117–24. Cambridge, MA: MIT Press.

León, Jorge. 2010. "Las Organizaciones Indígenas y el Gobierno de Rafael Correa." *Íconos: Revista de Ciencias Sociales* 37: 13–23.

Lepore, Jill. 2014. "The Disruption Machine: What the Gospel of Innovation Gets Wrong." *New Yorker*, June 23.

Lessig, Lawrence. 2001. *The Future of Ideas: The Fate of the Commons in a Connected World.* New York: Random House.

———. 2004. *Free Culture: How Big Media Uses Technology and the Law to Lock Down Culture and Control Creativity.* New York: Penguin.

Littlefield, Alice. 1978. "Exploitation and the Expansion of Capitalism: The Case of the Hammock Industry of Yucatan." *American Ethnologist* 5 (3): 495–508.

———. 1979. "The Expansion of Capitalist Relations of Production in Mexican Crafts." *Journal of Peasant Studies* 6 (4): 471–88.

Lyon, Sarah. 2011. *Coffee and Community: Maya Farmers and Fair Trade Markets.* Boulder: University of Colorado Press.

Mains, Daniel. 2012. "Blackouts and Progress: Privatization, Infrastructure, and a Developmentalist State in Jimma, Ethiopia." *Cultural Anthropology* 27 (1): 3–27.

Malinowski, Bronislaw. 1984. *Argonauts of the Western Pacific.* Prospect Heights, IL: Waveland Press.

Malinowski, Bronislaw, and Julio de la Fuente. 1982. *Malinowski in Mexico: The Economics of a Mexican Market System.* London: Routledge & Kegan Paul.

Martin, Ron, and Peter Sunley. 2003. "Deconstructing Clusters: Chaotic Concept or Policy Panacea?" *Journal of Economic Geography* 3 (1): 5–35.

Martínez Valle, Luciano. 2003. "Los Nuevos Modelos de Intervención sobre la Sociedad Rural: De la Sostenibilidad al Capital Social." In *Estado, Etnicidad y Movimientos Sociales en América Latina*, edited by Víctor Bretón and Francisco García, 129–58. Barcelona: Icaria.

Martínez Valle, Luciano, and Liisa L. North. 2009. *"Vamos Dando la Vuelta." Iniciativas Endógenas de Desarrollo Local en la Sierra Ecuatoriana*. Quito, Ecuador: FLACSO-Sede Ecuador.

Marx, Karl. 1963 [1852]. *The Eighteenth Brumaire of Louis Bonaparte*. New York: International Publishers.

Mayer, Enrique José, and Manuel Glave. 1999. *"Alguito para Ganar* (A Little Something to Earn): Profits and Losses in Peasant Economies." *American Ethnologist* 26 (2): 344–69.

McCann, Philip, and Stephen Sheppard. 2003. "The Rise, Fall and Rise Again of Industrial Location Theory." *Regional Studies* 37 (6): 649–63.

McCay, Bonnie, and James M. Acheson, eds. 1987. *The Question of the Commons*. Austin: University of Texas Press.

Meisch, Lynn A. 2002. *Andean Entrepreneurs: Otavalo Merchants and Musicians in the Global Arena*. Austin: University of Texas Press.

Meisch, Lynn A., and Rudi Colloredo-Mansfeld. 2007. "Belt Weaving in Ariasucu, Otavalo Area, Imbabura Province." In *Weaving and Dyeing in Highland Ecuador*, edited by Ann Pollard Rowe, Laura M. Miller and Lynn A. Meisch, 244–50. Austin: University of Texas Press.

Milgram, B. Lynne. 2000. "Reorganizing Textile Production for the Global Market: Women's Craft Cooperatives in Ifugao, Upland Philippines." In *Artisans and Cooperatives: Developing Alternative Trade for the Global Economy*, edited by Kimberly M. Grimes and B. Lynne Milgram, 107–28. Tucson: University of Arizona Press.

Ministerio Coordinador de Patrimonio Natural y Cultural. 2009. Recupera el Patrimonio de la Provincia de Imbabura. Quito, Ecuador.

Montaner, Carlos Alberto. 2001. *Journey to the Heart of Cuba: Life as Fidel Castro*. New York: Algora Publishing.

Movimiento Alianza PAIS. 2013. Programa de Gobierno 2013–2017: 35 Propuestas para el Socialismo del Buen Vivir. Quito, Ecuador.

Murra, John V. 1962. "Cloth and Its Functions in the Inca State." *American Anthropologist* 64 (4): 710–28.

Nash, June, ed. 1993. *Crafts in the World Market: The Impact of Global*

Exchange on Middle American Artisans. Albany: State University of New York Press.

Navarro, Vicente. 2002. "A Critique of Social Capital." *International Journal of Health Services* 32 (3): 423–32.

Nonini, Donald M., ed. 2007. *The Global Idea of "the Commons."* New York: Berghahn Books.

Ostrom, Elinor, Thomas Dietz, Nives Dolsak, Paul C. Stern, Susan Stonich, and Elke U. Weber, eds. 2002. *The Drama of the Commons.* Washington, DC: National Academies Press.

Paredes, César. 2010. "Clusters y Desarrollo Local: El Caso del Distrito Textil en Atuntaqui." *Eutopía* 1: 101–12.

Paxson, Heather. 2013. *The Life of Cheese: Crafting Food and Value in America.* Berkeley: University of California Press.

Piore, Michael J., and Charles F. Sabel. 1984. *The Second Industrial Divide: Possibilities for Prosperity.* New York: Basic Books.

Plattner, Stuart. 1996. *High Art Down Home: An Economic Ethnography of a Local Art Market.* Chicago: University of Chicago Press.

Popkin, Samuel L. 1979. *The Rational Peasant: The Political Economy of Rural Society in Vietnam.* Berkeley: University of California Press.

Porter, Michael E. 1998. "Clusters and the New Economics of Competition." *Harvard Business Review* 76 (6): 77–90.

Portes, Alejandro. 1998. "Social Capital: Its Origins and Applications in Modern Sociology." *Annual Review of Sociology* 24: 1–24.

Posso Yépez, Miguel Ángel. 2008. *Fábrica Textil Imbabura ¡La Historia! y los Acontecimientos Más Relevantes de Antonio Ante.* Ibarra and Atuntaqui, Ecuador: Pontifica Universidad Catolica Ecuador-Sede Ibarra.

Poster, Winifred R. 2002. "Racialism, Sexuality, and Masculinity: Gendering 'Global Ethnography' of the Workplace." *Social Politics* 9 (1): 126–38.

Prieto, Mercedes. 2011. "Indigenous Citizenship: Public Women, Language, and Handicrafts in Ecuador, 1941–1952." *Latin American and Caribbean Ethnic Studies* 6 (1): 27–46.

Putnam, Robert D. 1995. "Tuning in, Tuning Out: The Strange Disappearance of Social Capital in America." *PS: Political Science and Politics* 28 (4): 664–83.

Raustiala, Kal, and Christopher Jon Sprigman. 2006. "The Piracy Paradox: Innovation and Intellectual Property in Fashion Design." *Virginia Law Review* 92 (8): 1687–777.

Reid, Herbert, and Betsy Taylor. 2010. *Recovering the Commons: Democracy, Place, and Global Justice.* Urbana: University of Illinois Press.

Reinhardt, Nola. 1988. *Our Daily Bread: The Peasant Question and Family Farming in the Colombian Andes*. Berkeley: University of California Press.

Ribadeneira de Casares, Mayra. 1990. *Tigua: Arte Primitivista Ecuatoriano*. Quito: Centro de Arte Exedra.

Richardson, David M., ed. 2011. *Fifty Years of Invasion Ecology: The Legacy of Charles Elton*. Hoboken, NJ: Wiley-Blackwell.

Richardson, David M., Petr Pyšek, and James T. Carlton. 2011. "A Compendium of Essential Concepts and Terminology in Invasion Ecology." In *Fifty Years of Invasion Ecology: The Legacy of Charles Elton*, edited by David M. Richardson, 409–20. Hoboken, NJ: Wiley-Blackwell.

Roca, Albert. 2002. "Capital Social y Desarrollo en las Comunidades Africanas, ¿Reto o Espejismo?" *Studia Africana* 13: 5–17.

Roces, Mina, and Louise Edwards. 2007. "Trans-National Flows and the Politics of Dress in Asia and the Americas." In *The Politics of Dress in Asia and the Americas*, edited by Mina Roces and Louise Edwards, 1–18. Portland, OR: Sussex Academic Press.

Rosen, Sherwin. 1981. "The Economics of Superstars." *American Economic Review* 71 (5): 845–58.

Rotherham, Ian D., and Robert A. Lambert, eds. 2011. *Invasive and Introduced Plants and Animals: Human Perceptions, Attitudes and Approaches to Management*. New York: Earthscan.

Rovine, Victoria L. 2008. *Bogolan: Shaping Culture through Cloth in Contemporary Mali*. Bloomington: Indiana University Press.

Salazar-Sutil, Nicolás. 2009. "What's in Your Wardrobe, Mr. Morales? A Study in Political Dress." *Popular Communication* 7 (2): 63–78.

Sarabino Muenala, Zoila. 2007. "El Proceso de Constitución de las Élites Indígenas en la Ciudad de Otavalo." Master's thesis, Facultad Latinoamericano de Ciencias Sociales—Quito.

Scott, James C. 1976. *The Moral Economy of the Peasant: Rebellion and Subsistence in Southeast Asia*. New Haven: Yale University Press.

Seligmann, Linda J. 2004. *Peruvian Street Lives: Culture, Power, and Economy among Market Women of Cuzco*. Urbana: University of Illinois Press.

Sennett, Richard. 2008. *The Craftsman*. New Haven: Yale University Press.

———. 2012. *Together: The Rituals, Pleasures and Politics of Cooperation*. New Haven: Yale University Press.

Shuman, Michael H. 2006. *The Small-Mart Revolution: How Local Businesses Are Beating the Global Competition*. San Francisco: Berrett-Koehler Publishers.

———. 2012. *Local Dollars, Local Sense: How to Shift Your Money from Wall Street to Main Street and Achieve Real Prosperity.* White River Junction, VT: Chelsea Green Publishing Company.

Simmel, Georg. 1997. "The Philosophy of Fashion." In *Simmel on Culture: Selected Writings*, edited by David Frisby and Mike Featherstone, 187–205. Thousand Oaks, CA: Sage Publications.

Smith, Adam. 1981 [1776]. *An Inquiry into the Nature and Causes of the Wealth of Nations.* 2 vols. Indianapolis: Liberty Fund.

———. 1982 [1759]. *The Theory of Moral Sentiments.* Indianapolis: Liberty Fund.

Smith, Carol A. 1978. "Beyond Dependency Theory: National and Regional Patterns of Underdevelopment in Guatemala." *American Ethnologist* 5 (3): 574–617.

———. 1984a. "Does a Commodity Economy Enrich the Few While Ruining the Masses? Differentiation among Petty Commodity Producers in Guatemala." *Journal of Peasant Studies* 11 (3): 60–95.

———. 1984b. "Forms of Production in Practice: Fresh Approaches to Simple Commodity Production." *Journal of Peasant Studies* 11 (4): 201–21.

Steiner, Christopher B. 1994. *African Art in Transit.* New York: Cambridge University Press.

Stephen, Lynn. 1991. *Zapotec Women.* Austin: University of Texas Press.

Stoll, David. 2010. "A Mayan Financial Crash: The Case of Nebaj." *ReVista: Harvard Review of Latin America* Fall, http://www.drclas .harvard.edu/publications/revistaonline/fall-2010-winter-2011/mayan -financial-crash.

———. 2013. *El Norte or Bust! How Migration Fever and Microcredit Produced a Financial Crash in a Latin American Town.* Lanham, MD: Rowman & Littlefield Publishers.

Taleb, Nassim Nicholas. 2007. *The Black Swan: The Impact of the Highly Improbable.* New York: Random House.

———. 2012. *Antifragile: Things That Gain from Disorder.* New York: Random House.

Taussig, Michael. 1980. *The Devil and Commodity Fetishism in South America.* Chapel Hill: University of North Carolina Press.

Tax, Sol. 1953. *Penny Capitalism: A Guatemalan Indian Economy.* Washington, DC: Smithsonian Institution, Institute of Social Anthropology.

Thompson, E. P. 1993. *Customs in Common: Studies in Traditional Popular Culture.* New York: The New Press.

Tice, Karin E. 1995. *Kuna Crafts, Gender, and the Global Economy*. Austin: University of Texas Press.

Torres Mejia, Patricia. 2010. "Corporation: A Peasant Strategy for their Relationship with the Changing Global Order." Paper presented at the annual meetings of the American Anthropological Association, New Orleans, Louisiana, November 17–21.

Trouillot, Michel-Rolph. 1986. "The Price of Indulgence." *Social Analysis* 19: 85–90.

———. 2003. *Global Transformations: Anthropology and the Modern World*. New York: Palgrave Macmillan.

van den Berghe, Pierre L. 1993. "Tourism and the Ethnic Division of Labor." *Annals of Tourism Research* 19 (2): 234–49.

Verdery, Katherine, and Caroline Humphrey. 2004. "Introduction: Raising Questions about Property." In *Property in Question: Value Transformation in the Global Economy*, edited by Katherine Verdery and Caroline Humphrey, 1–25. New York: Berg.

Visser, Evert-Jan. 1995. "Limits to Local Learning: The Case of a Spatial Cluster of Small Clothing Manufacturing Firms in Lima Peru." Paper presented at Latin American Studies Association Congress, Washington, DC.

Weber, Max. 1958. *The Protestant Ethic and the Spirit of Capitalism*. Translated by Talcott Parsons. New York: Charles Scribner's Sons.

Weismantel, Mary J. 1988. *Food, Gender, and Poverty in the Ecuadorian Andes*. Philadelphia: University of Pennsylvania Press.

Whitten, Norman E. 2004. "Ecuador in the New Millennium: 25 Years of Democracy." *Journal of Latin American Anthropology* 9 (2): 439–60.

Whyte, William Foote. 1975. "Conflict and Cooperation in Andean Communities." *American Ethnologist* 2 (2): 373–92.

Winslow, Deborah. 2009. "The Village Clay: Recursive Innovations and Community Self-Fashioning among Sinhalese Potters." *Journal of the Royal Anthropological Institute* 15 (2): 254–75.

Wolf, Eric R. 1966. *Peasants*. Englewood Cliffs, NJ: Prentice-Hall.

———. 1969. *Peasant Wars of the Twentieth Century*. New York: Harper and Row.

Wood, W. Warner. 2008. *Made in Mexico: Zapotec Weavers and the Global Ethnic Art Market*. Bloomington: Indiana University Press.

Yanagisako, Sylvia Junko. 2002. *Producing Culture and Capital: Family Firms in Italy*. Princeton: Princeton University Press.

Index

marketplace and, 96–97; as part of
past, 25; politics of, 30
communities: artisans as respond-
ing to demand of, 33, 35–36; big
winners in, 91–92; competition
and, 64–65; governance of natural
resources by, 30; historically
invaded, 28; invasive trades in,
185–186; products as ties of, 62;
social capital and conflict in, 128
competition: for artisan crafts, 63;
in artisan life, 37; bid-to-the-
bottom cycle of, 145–146, 194;
cluster development and, 122–123;
destructive, 194; disloyal, 31, 64,
95, 115, 190; dynamics of, 64–65;
Expoferia trade show and, 138;
inequality of earnings and, 65–75,
66, 69, 71, 78; loyal, 190; predatory
copying and, 94–96, *95*; unfin-
ished business of, 84–88. *See also*
winner-take-all competition
consumer expectations of tradition, 35
Cook, Scott, 65, 76
copying: of designs in Otavalo, *95,*
95–96; of designs in Zuleta,
169–170; economics of, 108, 110;
predatory, 94–96, *95*, 115; of shirt
designs, 101–103, *104, 105*, 106, *107,*
108, *109*
Correa, Rafael: gifts of shirts by, 4,
170, 171–172; inaugural shirt of,
1–2, *3*, 10–11, 106, 108, 154–155, 157–
163, 170–171, 173–174; neoliberalism
and, 163; Plaza de Ponchos and,
19, 173; shirts of, 152–154, *153*, 155–
156, 170–172; Uribe and, 3–4
cottage industries, artisans as partici-
pating in, 33, 34
craft economies in Latin America, 18
cultural commons: designs as, 163–
170; economic stewardship and,

156; emergence of, 30–31; overview
of, 190–191; politics and, 156, 176;
shirts and, 174–176
cultural heritage projects in Atuntaqui, 140–141, 146, 150
cultural items, shirts and sweaters as,
110–114, *113*
cultural work of competition, 64–65
cuy, 8
Cuyo, Jaime, 67
Cuyo, Juan Luis, 74–75, 82–83, 84–85,
87, 88
Cuyo, Puri, 82–83

Dalmau, Francisco and Antonio,
130
Davidson, Adam, 23, 38, 187
de Janvry, Alain, 29
de la Torre, Carlos, 171
designs: copying of, *95*, 95–96, 169–
170; as cultural commons, 163–170;
cultural relevance of, 110–114, *113*;
as intellectual property, 108, 110,
160, 161–162; Jama Coaque culture
and, 159, 161, 169; ownership of,
155–156; public life of, 101–103, *104,*
105, 106, *107*, 108, *109*, 188–189; of
shirts, 12–14, *13*, 18–19, 157–163, 181;
of sweaters, 93–95, *94*; technology
and innovations in, 100, 101–102;
trends in, 114–116
differentiation in product lines, 103,
106
Dinero Rápido Fácil y Efectivo
(DRFE), 43
disruption and invasive trades, 182–
183
disruptive technologies, 5
dollarization, 2, 20, 70, 121
drug running, accusations of, 75–76
Durkheim, Emile, 51–52
Dyer, Jeff, 5